In Jesus and Mary

Fr Titus S.A.

Feb 8
1940

OUR LADY AND REUNION

Our Lady of the Atonement, Mother of Unity

Our Lady And Reunion

·

An Essay on the Role of
the Blessed Virgin Mary,
Queen and Mother of the World,
in Uniting All Mankind with God

·

by Titus F. Cranny, S.A., M.A., S.T.D.

Chair of Unity Apostolate
GRAYMOOR, GARRISON, N. Y.

Library of Congress Catalog Card Number 62-21829

Imprimi Potest: Bonaventure Koelzer, S.A., Superior General

Nihil Obstat: James Rigney, S.T.D., Censor Librorum

September 14, 1962

Imprimatur: ✠ Francis Cardinal Spellman, Archbishop of New York

Printed and bound in the United States of America
by Graymoor Press, Peekskill, N. Y.

To the devoted memory

of

FATHER PAUL JAMES FRANCIS, S.A.

and

MOTHER LURANA MARY FRANCIS, S.A.

who gave their religious communities and the

Catholic world this sacred legacy:

devotion to

OUR LADY OF THE ATONEMENT

Table of Contents

5

Introduction

Among Catholics, there has never been a greater interest in Mariology than at the present time. Devotion, theology, and the arts have combined to honor the Mother of God and the Mother of all men. The age of Mary, of which the saints have written, seems to have arrived.

On the other hand there has never been such a widespread interest in Christian Unity among non-Catholics. The meetings, discussions, mergers of various groups, and formation of councils are indicative of the spiritual phenomenon which characterizes our age. The Holy Office of the Catholic Church has issued an instruction on the Ecumenical Movement (1949) stating that: "Under the inspiring grace of God, due chiefly to the common prayers of the faithful, a desire has awakened and is growing daily in the hearts of many who are separated from the Catholic Church, that a reunion be accomplished among all who believe in Christ the Lord. Assuredly to the children of the true Church, this is a source of holy joy in the Lord as well as an inducement to lend their assistance to all who are sincerely seeking the truth, by entreating light and strength for them from God in fervent prayer."

At first glance, it might seem that there is little con-

7

nection between Our Lady and the Ecumenical Movement. But if we consider the matter briefly, we shall see that the connection is very clear and very real. Catholics hold that Our Lady is the special advocate before God in winning and dispensing grace to the souls of men. She intercedes for the welfare of the world. She prays unceasingly for the cause of Unity with the voice and accents of a loving Mother.

The Catholic theologian, Fr. Walter Burghart, S.J., has appraised the situation in this way: "Unless we confront the problem that is of prime concern . . . we shall go on talking to ourselves. Not a bad thing, this talking to ourselves; a generation ago we did not even do that. Not a bad thing, but not adequate to the contemporary crisis, to the temper of our times, to the ecumenical situation. This new concentration will involve intellectual agony; . . . It may well involve spiritual agony; for our discoveries may shake our complacencies. But the experience should be intellectually and spiritually stimulating—for ourselves, and for those not of our number to whom we say so insistently that the function of Our Lady, in the twentieth century, as in the first, is to bring God down to men and men up to God.'"

Pope John has repeatedly called attention to the role of Our Lady in the matter of Unity. "The modern development of Mariology and Marian piety in the Church," he has said, "is the surest sign and the happiest forecast that Mary is the greatest help offered us by God for the attainment of unity." The coming Vatican Council will open on the feast of the Maternity of Our Lady, October 11, to beg her guidance and protection, to pay tribute to her Motherhood of God and to recall the glory of Ephesus in 431. "Ours is a Marian Age," Pope John said, "and it becomes more evident day by day that the way for men to return to God is by Mary; that Mary is the basis of our confidence, the guarantee of our security, and the founda-

8

tion of our hope." He has asked the faithful to pray to Our Lady for the success of the Council, which will deal, at least indirectly, with the great matter of Christian Unity.

On the other hand, non-Catholics consider the Blessed Virgin as a great obstacle to religious unity. They hold that the Catholic concept of Our Lady creates a barrier of insuperable proportions, or in the words of Max Thurian: "Mariology poses the most agonizing problem of ecumenical thought." They believe that Catholic devotion to Mary makes religious unity impossible of achievement.

But in either case, Our Lady is to be reckoned with. For Catholics, she is the special patroness; for non-Catholics, the great obstacle.

Our thesis in presenting this work is that Our Lady is indeed *Mater unitatis*, the Mother of Unity, as St. Augustine has said, constantly praying for the unity of all men in the one Church of her beloved Son. We shall present the Catholic teaching, taken principally from the writings of recent popes. We shall also consider the position of those who view Our Lady in a different way, not in the spirit of hostility or argumentation, but to indicate what their position is and to show why, in their eyes, it presents such a problem. In this matter we recall the words of Pope Pius XII in *Humani generis* that "Catholic theologians have a grave responsibility of defending truth, both human and divine, and for instilling it into men's minds; they must needs acquaint themselves with all these speculations, to a more or less extent erroneous; they must needs take them into account. Nay, it is their duty to have a thorough understanding of them. There is no curing a disease unless you have a study of its symptoms..."

Throughout history Our Lady has always been a challenge. She has aroused sentiments of deepest love and of vehement hostility; rarely has her name left men of strong religious convictions neutral or impassive. Indeed, the reaction to her name and personality has often been the touchstone of the Catholic faith. For example, during the Christmas season of 1958 in South Africa, a Christmas seal was circulated in order to raise money for an anti-tuberculosis campaign. It was a picture of Our Lady and the Christ Child. But it had to be withdrawn because of complaints made by members of the Dutch Reformed Church who considered the seal as "offensive to Protestants and to the scriptural point of view" because it showed Our Lady with a halo larger than that of the Divine Infant. "The figure of Mary, mother of Jesus," they said, "is a special one for all Christians. She is mentioned in the Bible as a blessed woman. But the reformed Christian does not share the view of the Roman Catholic Church, which has bestowed on her a homage equal to that paid to the Saviour, such as represented on this stamp."

This judgment made on Catholic devotion and teaching is quite inaccurate, although the incident bears out the point that Our Lady is indeed a matter of contention for those outside the Church. The role of the Blessed Virgin in the sanctification and salvation of men cannot be ignored or minimized; it must be properly known and appreciated; so also must her role as Mother of Unity.

Indeed as Fr. John A. Hardon, S.J., has said: "Mary and the acceptance of all the great prerogatives by which the Church honors her ... form the test of the Christian religion." Our Lady is a challenge to our separated brethren and "In the degree which a person believes that Mary was immaculately conceived, that she is the Mother of God, and is now gloriously reigning in heaven, body and soul, interceding for us with her Divine Son, to that extent he is a true Christian. Insofar as he deviates from these Marian doctrines and, worse still, shows himself hostile to us who believe in them, we do not question his sincerity, but we say that he has departed from the Gospel

10

of Christ and is alien to its spirit of Christianity." Thus, Our Lady is a test of the Catholic faith and the norm of true doctrine.

This emphasis upon her part in the apostolate of Christian Unity is not a new role. At the very beginning of the Church the Holy Spirit descended upon the apostles in the upper room who were "with Mary, the Mother of Jesus". During the first centuries of the Christian era, the Church was struggling against the power of pagan emperors, battling against religious error and upholding the purity of the faith. From early times the triumphant words of the Irish poet, Sedulius, have echoed through the Church and been incorporated into its liturgy: "*Gaude, Virgo Maria, cunctas hereses sola interemisti in universo mundo*—Rejoice, O Virgin Mary, thou alone hast destroyed all heresies throughout the world." Our Blessed Mother preserves the members of Christ in the purity of the faith as she did long ago; she enables men to overcome temptations against it; and she exercises the functions of spiritual Mother and gracious Queen in the giving and strengthening of the faith among her children.

With his usual clarity and incisiveness Cardinal Newman has cited the function of devotion to Mary and its relation to the Church and Our Lord. "It is customary with those who are not Catholics to fancy that the honors we pay to Mary interfere with the supreme worship we pay to Him; that in Catholic teaching she eclipses Him. But this is the very reverse of the truth. For if Mary's glory is so very great, how can not His be greater still who is the Lord and God of Mary? He is infinitely above His Mother; and all that grace which filled her is but the overflowings and superfluities of His incomprehensible sanctity. And history teaches us the same lesson. Look at the Protestant countries which threw off all devotion to her three centuries ago, under the notion that to put her from their thoughts would be exalting the praises of her Son. Has that consequence really followed from their profane conduct towards her? Just the reverse—the countries, Germany, Switzerland, England, which so acted, have in great measure ceased to worship Him, and have given up their belief in His divinity; while the Catholic Church, wherever she is to be found, adores Christ as true God and true Man, as firmly as ever she did; and strange indeed would it be, if it ever happened otherwise."

A century ago, Fr. Frederick Faber laid bare the tragic results of a weak devotion to the Mother of God, His observation was about his own country of England, but with proper qualifications, his words apply to every part of the Catholic world at any time. "Devotion to Our Lady is low and thin and poor. It has no faith in itself. Hence, it is that Jesus is not loved, that heretics are not converted, that the Church is not exalted, that souls that might be saints wither and dwindle, that the sacraments are not rightly frequented or souls enthusiastically evangelized. Thousands of souls perish because Mary is withheld from them. It is the miserable unworthy shadow which we call our devotion to the Blessed Virgin that is the cause of all these wants and blights, these evils and omissions and declines. Yet, if we are to believe the revelations of the saints, God is pressing for a greater, a wider, a stronger, quite another devotion to His Blessed Mother."

Contrariwise, we may say the genuine love of Our Lady produces wonderful results in the Christian life. It increases zeal, charity, the spirit of simplicity and love of poverty among souls. It is an integral part of our holy faith. Through Mary souls are won back to the sacraments and unbelievers are brought to the waters of baptism. Jesus is magnified because Mary is glorified. Jesus is known because Mary is preached to men. The words of Dante well express the spirit of Our Lady's greatness:

O Virgin Mother, Daughter of Thy Son
Created beings all in lowliness
Surpassing, as in heights above them all
Termed by the 'ternal counsel pre-ordained,
Ennobler of thy nature, so advanc'd
In thee, that its great Maker did not scorn
Himself in His own work enclos'd to dwell;
For in thy womb rekindling shone the love
Reveal'd whose genial influence makes now
This flower to germin in eternal peace!
Here thou to us, of charity and love
Art, as the noon-day torch; and art, beneath
To mortal men, of hope a living spring.

So mighty art Thou, Lady! and so great
That he who grace desireth, and comes not
To thee for aidence, fain would have desire
Fly without wings. Not only him who asks
Thy bounty succors, but aidence doth freely oft
Forerun the asking. Whate'er may be
Of excellence in creature, pity mild,
Relenting mercy, large munificence,
Are all combined in thee.
                    (Paradiso, c. 33, Carey trs.)

All the graces of heaven, all the favors of God come
to man through the hands and heart of Our Lady. All hope
of eternal life, all achievement in striving after virtue, all
success in winning souls for God, come in the way that
Divine Wisdom has planned it—through Our Lady. No wonder that St. Bernard of Toledo could cry those beautifully
bold words: "For thy sake, O Mary, the Scriptures were
written, because of thee the world was made!"

We hope this modest treatise on Our Lady and Reunion will contribute in some small way to a deeper awareness of Mary's role in the work of winning souls to the

love of her Son and to membership in the Church. For as Pope Leo XIII has said: "It is impossible to think of any individual who has ever contributed or ever will contribute as much service towards the reconciliation of men with God as Mary."

The motivation and the inspiration for this work has been the great and gentle priest who is my religious founder, Fr. Paul James Francis, S.A. His desire for unity was all-consuming; his love for the Blessed Virgin, whom he singularly honored as Our Lady of the Atonement, was an ever-present element in his spiritual life and in his apostolate. Together with Mother Lurana Mary Francis, S.A., foundress of the Atonement Sisters, he began this Marian title and devotion which has spread over much of the Catholic world. May his spirit enkindle within human hearts a fitting knowledge and love of Our Lady, and may her benign influence as Mother and Queen spread ever more widely among the souls of men.

"That all may be one"—through Mary.

Feast of Our Lady of the Atonement

July 9, 1962

One ❧ Presenting the Background

"Mary is the greatest help offered us by God for the attainment of unity."

—Pope John XXIII.

The Catholic Church looks upon Our Lady through the eyes of Pope Pius IX, who in his declaration of the dogma of the Immaculate Conception said: "We repose with absolute confidence in the certitude of our hopes: the Blessed Virgin Immaculate who crushed the serpent's head, will through her powerful patronage, bring it to pass that all obstacles being removed, all errors vanquished, the Holy Catholic Church will grow stronger everywhere and flourish more and more among all peoples in all countries—it will reign everywhere so that there will be but one fold and one shepherd."

The role of our Lady in the redemptive work of Christ and in the redemptive mission of the Church is becoming more appreciated. The Age of Mary is the era of the apostolate; and in the providence of God this period in history will be the Age of Unity. Such was the strong conviction of Father Paul of Graymoor, when he spoke of Christian reunion and religious unity. He was certain that this great spiritual blessing would come about through the intercession and love of the Blessed Virgin Mary. Thus he spoke of Mary as Our Lady of the Atonement to emphasize her role in the mystery of Calvary; but he gave an extended meaning to this Atonement title. He said it also means Our Lady of the At-one-ment, Our Lady of Unity.

This modern Poverello seems to have followed implicitly the teaching of St. Irenaeus: the concept of re-uniting all men in Christ; of losing everything in Adam, of re-gaining all in Christ; of man being separated by Adam's fall and of being made at-one with God through the atoning act of the Son of God upon the altar of the Cross. Our Lady revealed to St. Bridget of Sweden the inseparable bond between Son and Mother: "Boldly assert that His suffering became my suffering, because His heart was mine. And just as Adam and Eve sold the world for an apple, so in a certain sense, my Son and I redeemed the world with one Heart."

When we speak of Our Lady's relationship to the Incarnation, we think in terms of its redemptive character. The whole life of Mary was sealed by the Atonement, which reached its climax in the Sacrifice of the Cross. In a great encyclical on Our Lady, Pope Leo XIII declared: "When Mary submitted as God's handmaid to undertake the office of Mother and when she offered herself with him in the temple, she was already a sharer with Him in His painful expiation on behalf of the human race ... 'There stood by the Cross of Jesus His Mother', who, moved by her unbounded charity to accept us as her sons, willingly offered with her Son the divine justice, dying with Him in her heart, pierced by the sword of sorrow."

The teaching on the Blessed Virgin as Our Lady of the Atonement is based on three prerogatives or offices. First, on her office as Co-Redemptrix, by which she shared in an incomparable way in the Sacrifice of her Son, and

16

by union with Him reconciled man to God and made atonement for sin, though in a dependent, auxiliary and subordinate way. In her own role she merited for men, satisfied for them. The very title of Our Lady of the Atonement points to this truth.

Secondly, by virtue of her power of intercession, Mary may be said to have a real part in regenerating men into the supernatural life of grace. She became the Mother of all men by virtue of the Incarnation, and particularly because of the Cross, when Jesus said: "behold thy Son . . . behold thy Mother." For Mary is a type of the Church, and just as men are said to be born of the Church, so also may they be said to be born supernaturally of Mary. This office is the spiritual Motherhood of Mary.

Thirdly, Mary presents to God the desires and prayers of men and obtains from Him divine benefits and blessings. This behooves her as Mother and associate with Christ in the mystery of the Cross, whereby all grace was gained for men. Thus, Mary is the Dispenser of all grace. Surely, then, if all graces come from the hands of Mary, that special grace of being a member of the Church or of becoming a member of it, comes from Our Lady.

This particular concept of Mary as Our Lady of the Atonement is not something novel; we have not discovered a new aspect of Marian theology in the twentieth century. It is new as a title, but its theological truths are rooted in tradition and in the teachings of the Church reaching back to the very first ages of the Christian faith. It emphasizes two phases of Marian teaching: first, Mary as the *Socia Christi* and *Co-Redemptrix mundi,* Associate of Christ and Co-Redemptrix of the world; and secondly, Mary as *Mater Unitatis,* Our Lady or Mother of Unity.

St. Epiphanius, Bishop of Constantinople in the sixth century, in writing to Pope Hormisdas said that the faithful should pray that the "unity of the Church may be preserved by the prayer of Mary, Our Lady, the holy and glorious Virgin and Mother of God."

We use the title of the Atonement to give special emphasis to the part that Mary plays in the lives of all men. When we consider this truth in a new light or from a different point of view, it takes on more profound meaning and significance. Thus the Mother of God had always been Our Lady of the Atonement because of her close association with and participation in the mystery of Calvary's Cross, and because of her unique function of bringing men to Christ and of uniting them to Him. Calvary has ever been the sacrifice of Unity by which man and God were made at-one through the outpouring of the Saviour's Blood which cleansed the world of sin. Through Father Paul and Mother Lurana, the Founders of the Society of the Atonement at Graymoor, the title and meaning of the Atonement were given a new emphasis so that man might realize the infinite riches of God shown forth in His Son and the unlimited glories of His lovely Mother. As St. Anselm wrote of Mary:

Mother of Justification and of the justified,
Mother of Reconciliation and of the reconciled,
Mother of Salvation and of the saved,
Mother of the Saviour and our Mother.

A recent author, Frank Sheed, expressed the meaning of Mary's role with Christ in the mystery of Calvary in these words: "God allowed that the suffering of the Divine Person would be accompanied by a wholly human suffering, as earnest as the suffering of redeemed humanity that was to be spread throughout the ages. As Christ represents humanity in the Redemptive Act, Mary represents humanity in the co-redemptive act. His suffering was the essential thing, and hers valuable only by derivation. His was the

18

Passion, hers the Co-Passion. He was the Redeemer but the Church loves to call her the Co-Redemptrix."

As Co-Redemptrix, Mary continues the work of the Redemptive Act by praying for the salvation of men, by interceding that they may become at-one with God, just as Our Lord continues His redemptive mission in the souls of the just, though He died upon the Cross nineteen centuries ago. Canon George Smith, in writing of Mary as Co-Redemptrix, commented:

> "Christ redeemed the human race by His Passion and death, in the sense that by His superabundant merit and atonement He reconciled man with God and made salvation possible for humanity. This He was able to do because as the Word Incarnate He is the supernatural Head of the human race, and therefore His merit and atonement avail condignly for all men who are mystically identified with Him. With His death on the Cross He concluded the first part of His redemptive work, the phase of *acquisition*. Having risen gloriously from the dead and ascended into heaven, He continues to the end of time to save the souls of men, interceding with the Father on our behalf and dispensing to us through His Sacred Humanity the gifts of grace which He has earned. This is the second phase of Redemption, the phase of *distribution*."

Our Lady of the Atonement continues as Mother and Mediatrix to exercise her role of dispensing grace to souls, to preserve their union with Christ and to unite to Him those who are separated by schism, heresy, indifference, neglect, or by any other sin. "Mary prays for the faithful that they may remain united to the Head of the Mystical Body whose members they are, and that they may continue to advance in justice and holiness. She prays for those outside the Church that they may hear the voice of the Good Shepherd and come into the one truefold."(Robellec: *Mystery of Divine Grace*).

Mary's role in the unity of all men with Christ is a development of Mary's spiritual motherhood of all, for every person is either an actual or a potential member of the Mystical Body of Christ. All have been reconciled to God by the suffering and death of the Redeemer; but they are not all formally reconciled so as to be actual members of the Church and children of Mary, in the sense of receiving grace from her and of receiving the benefits which membership in the Church confers.

Mary likewise has a special interest in souls as a result of her participation in the Atonement, for she not only prays and intercedes for men, but she truly suffered for the salvation of all men in a secondary way, united with and dependent upon the sacrifice of her Son. Because she suffered for men the pangs of spiritual birth, she is vitally interested in every soul. "Can a mother forget the child of her womb?" That is why, in a sense, every sin, because it is an affront to the majesty, love and mercy of God, is at the same time a rejection of Mary's love and a repudiation of her goodness. If Mary suffered for men, was spiritually crucified for them, and occupies a unique and unequalled position in the mystery of the Cross, then it follows that Mary suffers when men sin. Although sin is not an offense against Mary in the theological sense of sin, it makes her suffer in a mysterious way, analogous to the suffering of the Sacred Heart when Jesus is offended by sin.

As Mary's function is to unite man with Christ, she is eminently interested in persons becoming members of the One Church wherein alone this unity is found. As St. Augustine declares: "By her love, the Blessed Virgin brings forth the faithful as members of the Church." In his comprehensive study of the Mystical Body, Father Marsch, S.J., stresses

20

this point about Our Lady: "Her role like that of the Church is to give Christ; to be the Mother of Christians and the Spouse of the Spirit. As the Church is holy, she is holy; as the Church is preserved from all error, so she is preserved from fault—and the same pope who defined Papal Infallibility also defined the Immaculate Conception. As the Church is the only house of God, outside of which there is no salvation, so she is the gate of heaven through which all grace comes down to Christians. As the Church is all this exclusively for the benefit of men, so she is all this in order to be completely the Mother of Christ and of Christians. Moreover, as heresy has reproached belief in the Church as a belittling of devotion to Christ, it has cast the same reproach at piety towards the Blessed Virgin." (*Theology of the Mystical Body*)

The holiness of Mary partakes of and reflects the matchless perfection of her Son. Its excellence consists in uniting men to Christ and of uniting Christ to all men. This is her office, her role, her function as Mother. Mary is mediatrix with the Mediator, as Pope Leo XIII has affirmed: "No less truly and properly we may affirm that, by God's will, nothing whatever of the inexhaustible treasury of all grace which the Lord stored up, is imparted to us except through Mary; for 'grace and truth came by Jesus Christ' (Jn. 1:17). As no one can draw near to the Father on high except through the Son, so no one can draw near the Son except through His Mother." (*Octobri mense*)

Mary's mediation is not simply that of prayer and intercession, but of grace and merit. She is mediatrix not to keep men away from Christ, not to provide a barrier to union with God, not to make Him distant to men and their needs, but precisely to draw them closer to her Son, to facilitate this approach, to make it easier and more permanent. Mary is an incentive towards union with Christ. Mary is the Mother of Christ and of the Whole Christ, which includes all His members united to Him. Mary is the Mother of all men, the Mother of divine grace, the Refuge of sinners, the Comforter of the afflicted, the New Eve—true Mother of the Living, the universal and Catholic Mother, the perpetual Advocate for all men. As Pope Pius IX wrote in his encyclical on the Immaculate Conception: "Mary is the safest refuge and most faithful helper of all who are in danger, and the most powerful mediatrix and counsel of the whole world at the throne of her only-begotten Son . . . with her motherly soul she interests herself in our salvation and is solicitous about the whole human race." (*Ineffabilis Deus*)

The love of motherhood is inseparable from life and it is reflected in all creation. The love of a child for the mother who gave him birth, and the love of a man dying forgotten in the street for his mother whom he remembers above all else when life is ebbing away, testify to the reality and strength of a mother's love. Nor did God intend that the supernatural life should be less human than human life. On the contrary, the very elevation of the supernatural intensifies and purifies the love of a mother; for if human mothers love their children, how much more does their heavenly Mother love and cherish them. God places in the hearts of mothers qualities of love and tenderness unmatched in any other creature. Surely then He did not fail to instill this love into the heart and soul of the Mother of all men—a love and tenderness beyond comparison or comprehension.

Perhaps Mary's love for her children has seldom been more tenderly expressed than by these words of St. Bernardine, which he placed upon the lips of Christ hanging upon the Cross: "O, My sweetest Mother, the little flock of your children cannot now be deprived of Me, their Shepherd and Father, and you, their teacher and Mother. Many people are still to be won for Me through those who will proceed from your living womb ... most sweet Mother, you have access to the chamber of My heart so that coming in to Me and going out, your sons can carry out what you will and dispense it to your sons."

St. Bonaventure presented this thought in Augustinian form—the Mother of the Head is the Mother of the members. "Because the Virgin Mary conceived Him, Who is Head of all the elect and Whose members are the rest of the saved, she must have an immense charity and benevolence to love all the elect with a maternal affection."

St. Bernard, whose love of Mary is a byword in Catholic life, spoke of the power of Mary thus in a sermon for the feast of the Assumption: "Who could measure the length and breadth, the height and depth of thy mercy, O Blessed Virgin?" he asked. Then he answered: "By its length, it will help until the last day those who implore it. By its breadth, that mercy fills the earth. Its height ascends to the city on high to make good its losses. Its depth goes down to the lowest abysses, to set at liberty those who sit in darkness and in the shadow of death; for by thee, heaven has been filled, hell emptied, the ruins of the heavenly Jerusalem restored, Christian life given back to the unhappy beings in whom sin had killed it."

Father Edward Leen, the Irish spiritual writer, cited this connection between Mary and the Church. "Without Jesus no salvation, without Mary no Jesus, as without Mary it is impossible to have a knowledge of Jesus ... The cause of all the heresies that have ravaged the Church, the explanation of all failures in the spiritual life, can be traced to a lack of recognition of the spiritual maternity of Mary." (*Our Blessed Mother*) Thus the lack of love for Mary means absence of love for Christ and for His Church; conversely, a genuine love for the Mother of God is an unfailing means to a full-souled, complete devotion to Christ and His Mystical Body. Such is God's plan of salvation and sanctification for all men.

Mary's office, at the present time, and lasting until the end of the world, is to watch over the Church, the Mystical Body, as once she watched over and guided Christ when He lived upon this earth. "She, as others, came into this world to do a work", commented Cardinal Newman, "she had a mission to fulfill; her grace and her glory are not for her own sake, but for her Maker's; and to her is committed the custody of the Incarnation; that is her appointed office . . . As she was once on earth, and was personally the guardian of her Divine Child . . . so now, and to the last hour of the Church do her glories and the devotion paid her proclaim and define the right faith concerning Him as God and man." (*Disc. to Mixed Congregations*)

Another thought from the same learned Cardinal appraises Our Lady's dignity and grandeur in this light. "In order to do honor to Christ, in order to defend the true doctrine of the Incarnation, in order to secure a right faith in the manhood of the Eternal Son, the Council of Ephesus proclaimed the Virgin Mary to be the Mother of God. Thus all the heresies of that day, though opposed to each other, led in a most wonderful way to her exaltation, and the Council of Antioch led the Church to determine first, the conceivable greatness of a creature, and then the incommunicable dignity of the Blessed Virgin." (*Development of Doctrine*)

The unfolding of history reveals the tremendous influence of the Mother of God in the work of sanctification and salvation. Our Lady is stronger than the insidious craft of Satan, more powerful than nations girded in military might; she is more influential than all the social and economic reforms of nations because she is the Mother of God and the divinely chosen instrument of grace for all men. At times the spectre of sin may be appalling, and difficulties

24

so vast and so complex so as to give little hope for Christian reunion. But there is no reason for fear or doubt. "In the end my Immaculate Heart will triumph." And so it will, because God wills it, and because Divine Wisdom said there would be but One Fold and One Shepherd. In such an achievement our Blessed Mother will have a leading role.

Two ❧ *According to Recent Popes*

"There is no surer or easier way of uniting men with Christ than Mary."

—St. Pius X.

Our treatment of Our Lady and Reunion in this chapter will concern papal documents from the time of Pope Leo XIII to Pope John XXIII. Their statements furnish sound support to our thesis that religious unity will be achieved principally through the Blessed Virgin Mary. Pope Leo XIII has often been called "The Pope of the Rosary" for his many writings and allocutions on this Marian prayer. He may justly be cited also for his statements about Our Lady and the cause of unity. Repeatedly he referred to "the great part that the Blessed Virgin had in the expansion, combats and triumphs of the Catholic Faith," which "evinces clearly the divine plan in her regard and should awaken in all sincere men a great hope for an answer to their prayers."

Pope Leo XIII (1878-1903)

This great pontiff frequently stressed Mary's part in the spread of the Christian Faith and in the building up of the Mystical Body of Christ. "We must trust Mary and seek her aid, for she would do anything in her power to reawaken religion, to reconcile souls *by the profession of the same faith* in all Christian nations, and to unite all wills by the bond of perfect charity. The confirmation of this hope may be realized if the conviction of many Marian souls materializes. They believe that Mary, the Mother of mankind, will be the strong link which will bind the lovers of Christ as brothers, obedient to one Father, the Vicar of Christ on earth, the Pope of Rome." Most of his utterances referred to the reunion of the separated brethren of the East, the various Orthodox bodies. The principle that Mary is the special means for gaining unity applies to any person or group separated from the one Fold of Christ.

The faithful share in the unity of the Church and in unity with each other through the operation of Our Blessed Lady. Her function is both positive and negative: positive, to spread the faith, to extend and exalt the Church, and to bring souls to a closer union with Christ; negative, to combat error and to destroy the evils of schism and heresy and apostasy. In the words of this Pontiff:

It has been her unremitting concern to see to it that the Catholic faith stands firmly lodged in the midst of the people, there to thrive in its fertile and undivided unity. Many and well known are the proofs of her solicitude, manifested from time to time even in a miraculous manner. In times and places in which, to the Church's grief, faith languished in lethargic indifference or was tormented by the baneful scourge of heresy, our great and gracious Lady in her kindness was ever ready with her aid and comfort. Under her inspiration, strong with her might, great men were raised up—illustrious for their sanctity no less than for their apostolic spirit—to beat off the attacks of wicked

27

adversaries and to lead souls back into the virtuous ways of Christian life, firing them with a consuming love for the Church. (*Adjutricem populi*)

Then Pope Leo showed the results of fervent devotion to Our Lady. Through her the Fathers and Doctors of the Church received their inspiration; through her the Christian rulers and the Popes have overcome the enemies of the Church. "Love for Mary has been a precious and powerful bulwark of the faith from the beginnings of the Church, not only for the suffering and the poor, but for the Pontiffs and Christian rulers, for Fathers and Doctors of the Church, enabling them to devote their talents to the glory of God and the welfare of souls." The Holy Father stated expressly that the Rosary was instituted principally "to implore the protection of the Mother of God against the enemies of the Catholic Church." Pope Leo was the Lion of Rome who used the Rosary to overcome the enemies of the Church in Germany, France, Italy, and every other country. The Mother of God is also the heavenly force to unite those separated from her Son.

> Hence it is that the Church and the Fathers have given expression to their joy in Mary in words whose beauty equals their truth: "Hail, voice of the Apostles, forever eloquent, solid foundation of the faith, unshakeable pillar of the Church." (Akatistos Hymn in the Greek Church.) "Hail, thou through whom we have been enrolled as citizens of the one Holy Catholic and Apostolic Church" (St. John Damascene). "Hail, thou fountain, springing forth by God's design, whose rivers flowing over in pure and unsullied waves of orthodoxy put to flight the hosts of error" (St. Germanus of Constantinople). "Rejoice, because thou alone hast destroyed all the heresies of the world."

Other portions from the same document are of special importance in expressing the bond between Our Lady and Unity. At times Pope Leo's encyclicals seem to have been overlooked, and especially those that deal *ex professo* of Our Lady, as the Mother of Unity, but a study of them is rewarding and enlightening.

Remembering that her only-begotten Son prayed so earnestly to His Heavenly Father for the closest union among the nations whom He has called by the one Baptism to the one 'inheritance of salvation' (Heb. 1:14) bought for an infinite price, will she not, for that reason, see to it that all in His marvelous light will strive as *with one mind for unity?* And will it not be her wish to employ her goodness and providence to console the Spouse of Christ, the Church, through her long-sustained efforts in this endeavor, as well as to bring to *full perfection the boon of unity* among the members of the Christian family, which is the illustrious fruit of her Motherhood?

Mary is the bond uniting her children in obedience and love for the Sovereign Pontiff. Those who are not members of the Church cannot be her spiritual children in the full sense. But she effectively intercedes for those who are separated from Her Son, and she seeks to bring them to the unity of the One Fold. She is the spiritual Mother of those who are united with her Son in the Church and she is the Mother of the erring and wandering who are unhappily separated from Him.

Mary will be the *happy bond to draw together, with strong, yet gentle constraint,* all who love Christ, no matter where they may be, to form a nation of brothers

29

yielding obedience to the Vicar of Christ upon earth, the Roman Pontiff, their common father.

Icons of Mary brought from the East to Rome and to the West are a sign of mutual devotion and a symbol of unity. Love for Our Lady is the priceless blessing of all members of the Church and the spiritual bridge that will bring the separated brethren of the East to the unity of One Fold of the Saviour.

And we may add here a detail not foreign to our subject and reflecting further glory upon the Mother of God. It is common knowledge that, under the changing fortunes of time, great numbers of venerable images to Our Lady have been brought from the East to the West, most of them finding their way to Italy and to Rome. Our forebears received them with the deepest respect and venerated them with magnificent honors; and their descendants, emulating their piety, continue to cherish these images as highly sacred treasures. It is a delight for the mind to discover in this fact the approval and the favor of a mother wholly devoted to her children. For it seems to indicate that these images have been left in our midst as witnesses of the ages when the entire Christian family was held together by the ties of absolute unity, and as so many precious pledges of our common inheritance. The very sight of them must needs invite souls, as though the Virgin herself were bidding them to keep in devout remembrance those whom the Catholic Church calls with loving care back to the peace and the gladness which they enjoyed of old within her embrace.

The Holy Father referred to the grace won through the Rosary, calling Mary "the most zealous guardian of

Christian Unity". St. Dominic and other saints of God obtained victories over heresy through the Rosary. Father Paul of Graymoor, a modern apostle of unity, urged the praying of the Rosary, as we will later show, to win graces from God and obtain the blessing of religious unity for confused and erring souls. Not only is the Rosary a worthy prayer, but the "best and most effective way", said Pope Leo, to win the favor of Our Lady.

And so, in Mary, God has given us the most zealous guardian of Christian unity. There are, of course, more ways than one to win her protection by prayer, but for us, we think that the *best and most effective way to her favor lies in the Rosary.* Prayerful use of the Rosary will enable souls to grow in the love and likeness of Christ. *Mary is the bond uniting Christ to men and bringing men to Christ.* The sublimity of that double dignity, the fruits of the two-fold ministry, appear in a clear light when we think of Mary's share in the joyful, the sorrowful and the glorious mysteries of her Son.

Pope Leo XIII called the Rosary "the best prayer" to Mary for the cause of Christian Unity, for the Blessed Virgin is the Mother of all who are born spiritually in the Church of Christ. She efficaciously prays for all who are members of the Church, and for all who are separated from Her Son and the Church which He founded.

For that reason we say that *the Rosary* is by far the *best prayer by which we plead before her the cause of our separated brethren.* To grant a favorable hearing belongs properly to her office as spiritual Mother. For Mary has not brought forth—nor could she—those who are of Christ except in the one faith and in the one

31

same love for "Is Christ divided?" All must live the life of Christ in an organic unity in order to bring forth fruit to God in one same body. (Rom. 7:4). Every one of the multitudes, therefore, whom the mischief of calamitous events has stolen away from the unity, must be born again to Christ of the same Mother whom God has endowed with a never-failing fecundity to bring forth a holy people. And Mary longs to do this. God grant that they not refuse to comply with the burning desire of their merciful Mother but on the contrary give ear like men of good will, with a proper regard for their eternal salvation, to the voice, gently persuasive, which calls to them: "My little children of whom I am in labour again, until Christ be formed in you" (Gal. 4:19).

Pope Leo wrote fondly of the love of Mary for her children, for she longs with intense desire to bring them to the Church, since the evils of the world have taken them away from the one Church—and from Christ and His Mother. He noted the devotion of the East towards the Rosary in times past. Dominican Friars who worked among people of the Eastern Rites were called "Friars of Unity," and at one time they numbered more than six hundred members. But the Protestant revolt which sapped the strength of so many religious communities also affected this Apostolate for Unity. The Pope expressed his joy that the faithful planned to build a shrine in Achaia to Mary as Queen of the Most Holy Rosary. It would be a symbol of Unity and a means of unifying East and West in expressing love for the Mother of God.

Knowing what power Our Lady's Rosary possesses, not a few of our predecessors were at special pains to spread the devotion throughout the countries of the

East—in particular, Eugene IV in the Constitution *Adversperascentes,* issued in 1439, and later Innocent XII and Clement XI. By their authority, privileges of wide extent were granted to the Order of Preachers in favor of the Project. The hoped-for results were forthcoming, thanks to the energetic activity of the brethren of the Order, results to which many a bright record bears witness, although time and adversity have since raised great obstacles in the way of further progress.

In his concluding remarks, the Holy Father again exhorted the faithful to pray to Mary for the great cause of Christian Unity.

The love and influence of Mary will bring back the millions who are separated from her and from the Church. The East has always been noted for its love for Our Lady, even among the separated brethren. The Holy Father urged prayers during October, the month of the Rosary, for this great intention. He established a number of feasts of saints from the East, St. Ephrem, Sts. Cyril and Methodius, and St. Basil. He asked that the Novena of Pentecost be observed throughout the world for the cause of Unity. He wrote more than twelve letters on the Rosary, often mentioning Unity. To Our Lady he confided the task of establishing souls in Unity.

Well may all, shepherds and flocks alike, fly with fullest confidence to the protection of the great Virgin, especially next month (October). Let them not fail to call upon her name with one voice, beseeching her as God's Mother, publicly and in private, by praise, by prayer, by the ardor of their desire: "Show thyself our Mother". May her motherly compassion keep her whole family safe from every danger, lead them in the path of genuine prosperity, above all, *establish them in holy Unity.*

She looks upon Catholics of every nation with a kindly eye; where the bond of charity joins them together she makes them more ready, more and more determinded to uphold the honor of religion, which at the same time, brings upon the state the greatest blessings. May she look with utmost compassion upon those great and illustrious nations which are cut off from the Church, upon the noble souls who have not forgotten their Christian duty. May she inspire in them the most salutory desires, foster their holy aspirations, and bring them to happy completion.

The example and teaching of this Pope in love for the Rosary inspired the faithful to an appreciation of this most beloved of Marian prayers. It is the dearest and most universal prayer to our Heavenly Queen and Mother. It is the best way "to promote the welfare of the human race." Pope Julius III called the Rosary "the glory of the Church," and Pope Urban IV said that every day it obtains "fresh blessings for Christianity." Our Lady still acts through "the battalions which fight the battle of Christ, armed with His sacred mysteries and under the guidance of the heavenly Father." She is assuredly the bulwark of the faith and the patroness of Unity.

In the East, may that widespread devotion to her which dissident nations profess, as well as the countless glorious acts of their ancestors in her honor, effectively aid them. In the West, may the memory of her beneficent patronage stand the dissidents in good stead; with surpassing kindness she has, through many ages, manifested her approval of, and has rewarded the admirable devotion shown her among every class. May the peoples of the East and West, and all others wherever they may be, profit by the suppliant voice of Catholics united in prayer, and by our voice which will cry out to our last breath, "Show thyself a Mother!" (Sept. 5, 1895)

Pope Leo likewise stated that "It is mainly to expand the kingdom of Christ that we look to the Rosary for the most effective help. On many occasions, we have declared that the object which at the present time engrosses our most earnest attention, is their reconciliation to the Church of nations which have become separated from her. We recognize, at the same time, that the realization of our hopes must be sought chiefly in prayer and supplication addressed to Almighty God."

This Holy Father also wrote many letters to individual groups of Eastern dissidents, the Armenians, Greeks and Slavs, calling them back to the Church to which their ancestors had belonged and had lent lustre. Even a cursory reading of the documents of Pope Leo XIII reveals how earnestly and frequently he appealed to the dissidents to come to their true home, the Catholic Church. He showed too his confidence in Our Lady to effect such a long-desired achievement.

Pope Leo quoted the words of St. Augustine (*De Sancta Virginitate,* 6) about Mary's charity effecting the birth of Christ's members in the Church. "So may the most powerful Virgin Mary who in times past cooperated by charity that the faithful might be born in the Church be now the intermediary and mediatrix of our salvation." Elsewhere, he wrote that "the influence of Mary is responsible for the acquisition and salutary cultivation of the faith ... she who brought forth the author of the faith (Heb. 2:12) and was called blessed because of her own faith." (Lk. 1:45) These thoughts remind us of the expressions of the Fathers, who spoke of Mary's role in man's striving for eternal life. "Hail, *through you whom* we have been enrolled as citizens in the one, holy Catholic and Apostolic Church," asserted St. John Damascene; while St. Germanus of Constantinople declared that "No one, O most Holy Virgin, is filled with the knowledge of God except through you; no one is saved, O Mother of God, except through you."

When Pope Leo wrote to the Anglicans in 1895 about Unity, he concluded with the beautiful prayer whose authorship has been attributed to Cardinal Merry del Val: "O Blessed Virgin Mary, Mother of God, and our own most gentle Queen and Mother, look down in mercy upon England, your Dowry, and upon us all who greatly hope and trust in you. Through you Jesus, our Savior and our hope, was given to the world; and He has given you to us that we might hope still more. Plead for us thy children, whom you received and accepted at the foot of the Cross. O Sorrowful Mother, intercede for our Anglican brethren, that they may be united with us in the one true fold under the supreme shepherd, the Vicar of Thy Son. Pray for us, dear Mother, that by faith, fruitful in good works, we may all deserve to see and praise God together with thee in our heavenly home." It combines the twofold idea of Our Lady of the Atonement—Mary at the foot of the Cross, and the special intercessor for Unity. In 1897 he established the archconfraternity of Our Lady of Compassion, whose objective was to implore by constant prayer the return of England to the Church.

Pope Leo said that one of the two great aims of his pontificate was "to promote the reunion of all those who have fallen away from the Catholic Church either by heresy or by schism, since it is undoubtedly the will of Christ that all would be united in one flock under one Shepherd." He appointed a commission to promote the reconciliation of the separated brethren with the Church. When a group of Anglicans showed interest in unity, the Holy Father wrote a moving letter *Ad Anglos* to encourage the good will of the non-Catholics and to urge the faithful to pray for their compatriots. Shortly thereafter, in 1896, he affirmed the traditional teaching on Anglican orders; this too was an act of charity, inspired by love for the truth. The Commission did not survive the pope, but the Pentecost novena for the cause of Unity still continues, though it is not as widely observed as it should be. In these undertakings and in all projects Pope Leo placed his confidence in the Mother of God.

Thus this great pope emphasized the role of the Blessed Virgin in achieving religious unity. To reconcile the separated brethren with the Church was the express purpose of his pontificate, and while he did not succeed to the degree that he had hoped, he advanced the cause of unity notably and did much to prepare the way for subsequent efforts— through his all-embracing charity and through his love for Our Lady and her rosary. The following message, which he sent to the Marian Congress at Leghorn in 1895, is a fine epitome of his confidence in Our Lady to win her separated children to the One Fold:

The faith of Christ is one, when one shepherd governs
    the flock,
When one love gathers together the scattered nations.
O Virgin, be propitious, gaze down with kindly eye
    upon the wanderers
And deign to unite them under thine only Son.

Pope St. Pius X (1903-14)

The next Supreme Pontiff, St. Pius X indeed was not as prominent in his work for reunion as his predecessor, but his holiness and example and the great Marian encyclical, *Ad diem illum*, were no small contributions to the apostolate of Unity. "No one," he stated, "is more powerful

37

than the Virgin in uniting men with Christ. No one ever knew Christ so profoundly as she knew Him and no one can be a more competent guide and teacher in knowing Christ . . . There is no surer or easier way for uniting all persons with Christ than by Mary and obtaining the perfect adoption of the sons of God."

This saintly Pope did not write this document explicitly on Christian Unity, but he emphasized the principle of calling upon Mary, of confidently trusting her, of stressing her role in bringing souls to Christ. Grace comes to men through Mary. What greater grace can there be than an increase of holiness for those who are united to Christ as members of His Spotless Bride, the Church, or the blessing of membership in the Church for those who do not possess it? The greatest spiritual favor is the gift of faith, that is, of believing all that God has revealed on His authority, and this means membership in the Church of the Divine Redeemer, being united by bonds of faith, worship, and authority to the Church which He founded.

St. Pius expressed the connection between Mary's role in the Church and her participation in the Sacrifice of the Cross by using the terms "Co-minister of the Redemption and co-minister of the graces that we receive". "It is hardly possible," he stated, "to put into words the power and scope added to these offices of hers on the day that she was taken up to the company of her Son in the height of heavenly glory, to which the dignity and lustre of her merits entitled her. From then on, she began, by God's decree, to watch over the Church, to assist and cherish us as our Mother, so that she was the co-minister in effecting the sacrament of human redemption and likewise the co-minister of the graces to be distributed from that sacrament for all time, for almost an unlimited power had been given her."

In a letter to the faithful at the Eucharistic Congress of

Lourdes in July, 1914, he also wrote: "Never has Mary ceased to show that motherly love which till her last breath she poured forth so fully upon the Bride that her Divine Son purchased with His Precious Blood. It might indeed be said that her sole work was to care for the Christian people, to lead all minds to the love of Jesus and zeal for His service. May the Divine Author and Preserver of the Church look upon that noble part of His flock, which is afflicted today by so many calamities; may He stimulate the generous virtue and willingness of the good and, pouring out the fire of His love, revive the half-dead faith of those who now barely retain the name of Christian. This, in our fatherly love for the French people, we most earnestly ask of God through the Immaculate Virgin."

It is also significant that St. Pius X has been chosen patron of the Second Vatican Council. His entire life, and especially his pontificate, was the literal fulfillment of the motto he had chosen: "To restore all things in Christ". His greatness is illustrated by the touching story of a Hungarian of Rumanian Orthodox faith who came to see the Pope. When the Holy Father entered the audience chamber, the man was very nervous. His Holiness noticed his discomfort, came to him and asked: "What is the matter, my son?" "Holy Father, I am not Catholic, but Orthodox." The great Pope placed his arm about the shaking shoulders. "It makes no difference; Catholic or Orthodox; you are all my children." The happy sequel is that the man did not leave Rome until he was received into the Church.

Pope Benedict XV (1914-22)

During the reign of Pope Benedict XV, there were no special documents dealing with Our Lady and Unity, though this pontiff was surely interested in the cause of the reunion of the separated East. He displayed singular concern for Eastern rite Catholics and asked prayers for the separated brethren. He blessed the Chair of Unity Octave in February, 1916, and extended it to the universal Church.

In his *Motu proprio* of May 1, 1917, Pope Benedict stressed the importance of the East in these often-quoted words: "The Church of Jesus Christ, since she is neither Latin nor Greek nor Slav but Catholic, makes no distinction between her children, and these, whether they are Greeks, Latins, Slavs, or members of their national Groups, all occupy the same rank in the eyes of this Apostolic See." At the request of this Holy Father, an Oriental branch of the Society of Jesus was begun in 1920, and chapels have been provided in the Generalate and at the Gregorian University. Pope Benedict also established the Congregation of the Oriental Church in the Roman Curia.

Pope Pius XI (1922-39)

Other papal pronouncements give weight to the thesis that it is Mary who is the great patroness of Christian reunion. On the feast of the Epiphany (Jan. 6th) in 1928, Pope Pius XI published *Mortalium animos,* pointing out that it was impossible for the Catholic Church to take part, on equal footing, with any other religious body in discussions on Christian unity. It was an answer to the Congress of Lausanne, Switzerland, in 1927. The Church is one, just as Christ is one. Any religious body other than the Catholic Church is not founded by Christ, does not hold authority from Him, and consequently does not, of itself, lead men to eternal life with God. At the conclusion of this encyclical, the Holy Father besought the aid of Our Lady. "In behalf of which lofty intentions we invoke and we ask that you invoke the intercession of the Blessed Virgin Mary, Mother of Divine Grace, conqueror of all heresies, and Help of

Christians that soon may dawn that longed-for day when all will hear the voice of her Divine Son, 'Keeping the unity of the spirit in the bond of peace'."

In 1931, Pope Pius XI wrote an encyclical to commemorate the fifteenth centenary of the Council of Ephesus. At the end of the document he made this reference to Our Lady and the cause of Unity: "Under the auspices of the heavenly Queen, we desire all to beg for a very special favor of the greatest importance, that she who is loved and venerated with such ardent piety by the people of the East, may not permit that they should be unhappily wandering and still kept apart from the unity of the Church, and thus from her Son, whose Vicar we are ... Would, moreover, that very soon the happiest of days might dawn when the Virgin Mother of God, looking through her image so exquisitely worked in mosaic under Our predecessor, Sixtus III, in the Liberian basilica and restored by us to its original beauty, would see the separated children returning to venerate her with one mind and one faith."

Thus, we say that Mary is Our Lady of the At-one-ment, that her function of reconciliation did not cease with the mystery of the Cross, but continues through the ages. Her task is to bring men to Christ, to the unity of His Church, whether they are separated by some barrier of heresy or schism or indifference, or whether they are infidels with little opportunity of knowing Christ and His truth. Mary's apostolic mission extends the graces of the Atonement of her Son by giving them to the souls of men and by raising up missionaries to expand the boundaries of the Church and reap the harvest of souls for God.

Mary's role is an immediate consequence of her role as Co-Redemptrix of the human race, as Mediatrix and Distributor of all graces. She longs for men to come to salvation; that is her great desire. But her apostolic mission differs from that of other apostles because it is for all times and places and for all who are saved and sanctified. Her role is as universal as that of her Son. Mary received from God the mission of sanctifying and of saving all, so that all who labor for souls must look to her as their Mother and Leader.

Those who work and pray for Christian Unity must turn to her who was united to God in such a wonderful way, and who from this union with the Trinity is the Model and Patroness of all unity endeavors. More than any saint and more than all the saints, she desires that men may be one with Christ in His Church. It is Mary's office to begin the work of unity by giving the grace to men; to continue it by dispensing additional grace; and to perfect it so that being united with the Church upon earth, men will receive the unending happiness of heaven. As St. Louis—Marie de Montfort has written: "The strongest inclination of Mary is to unite us to Jesus Christ, her Son; and the strongest inclination of the Son is that we should come to Him through His Holy Mother."

On the third centenary of the death of St. Josaphat, martyr for reunion in 1623, Pope Pius XI wrote an encyclical to mark the anniversary. After reviewing the virtues of the saintly bishop, His Holiness urged the faithful to have recourse to prayer to Mary for the cause of Unity: "Let us invoke this most kind Mother, especially with this title, 'Queen of Pastures', that the straying brothers may return to the life-giving pastures where St. Peter, ever living in his successors and Vicar of the eternal Shepherd, feeds and guides all the lambs and sheep of the Christian flock".

Pope Pius XI promoted the cause of Unity unceasingly. He enhanced the works of his predecessors and urged the faithful of the West to learn more about the rites and history of the East. He did much for the missionaries in all parts of the world. As for those separated from Rome, the hope for their return lies in Mary, as the Pope said: "The

Orientals have scrupulously preserved so large a part of divine revelation, manifest such a sincere devotion to Christ our Lord, foster such a remarkable love and attachment to His Immaculate Mother and enjoy the real administration and reception of the sacraments."

Pope Pius XII (1939-58)

Pope Pius XII frequently called upon the power of Mary to heal the breach between the Eastern Separated Brethren and Rome. Notable among his statements were the two encyclicals: *"Orientalis Ecclesiae decus,* on the occasion of the fifteenth centenary of the death of St. Cyril of Alexandria (April 9, 1944): and the letter to the Russian people, July 7, 1952, at which time he consecrated their nation to the Immaculate Heart of Mary. In the first document he wrote:

> Indeed, to all alike we recommend in a particular way that most effective aid, which in any work for the saving of souls must take the first place both in order of time and efficacy; fervent, humble and confident prayer to God. And we should have them invoke the most powerful patronage of the Virgin Mother of God, that, through the gracious intercession of the most loving Mother of us all, the Divine Spirit may enlighten the minds of Eastern people with His heavenly light, and that all of us may be one in the one Church which Jesus Christ founded, and which the same Spirit, the Paraclete, nourishes with an unceasing shower of graces and stirs to sanctity.

The Holy Father also recommended the observance of Oriental Day in colleges and seminaries as a stimulus to a greater knowledge and love of the Eastern rites. He added: "... on that day let prayers more than usually fervent be made to the Divine Shepherd of the whole Church, and let the hearts of the young be stimulated to a burning zeal for the achievement of this holy unity."

In his letter to the people of Russia, of July 7, 1952, Pope Pius XII recalled the presence of the church of the Assumption within the very walls of the Kremlin as "most clear testimony of the affectionate devotion which your forbears and you have for the Beloved Mother of God. When Mary interposes her powerful protection against the forces of evil, she will prevail." Through prayer to Mary may the faith be strengthened, and the wiles of the enemies of religion driven away; the plans of the atheist be dissipated, that "She may deign to obtain for their minds that light which comes from on high and direct their hearts through divine grace unto salvation". Then he concluded the message with this thought:

And with the same suppliant appeal we pray the same most loving Mother that she may assist each and every one of you in the present calamitous circumstances and obtain from her Divine Son heavenly light for your minds, and for your souls that virtue and fortitude by which, with sustaining divine grace, you may be able to overcome impiety and error.

Pope Pius XII often called upon Our Lady as the Mediatrix of all graces, as the Associate with Christ in saving the human race; and on several occasions he spoke of the achievement of the unity of all who believe in Christ as Mary's special task. Thus, in the encyclical on the Marian year, *Fulgens corona* (1953), he referred to these words to Mary's power to win back the Eastern separated brethren and others separated from the Holy See:

... We call upon those who are separated from us by an ancient schism and whom, nonetheless, we love with paternal affection, to unity in pouring forth these joint prayers and supplications, knowing full well how greatly they venerate the Mother of Jesus Christ and celebrate her Immaculate Conception.

Then he turned to those "who are proud to call themselves Christians, and are united at least by the bond of charity":

May the same Blessed Virgin look down on all who are proud to call themselves Christians, and who, being united at least by the bond of charity, humbly raise to her their eyes, their minds and their prayers, imploring that light which illumines the mind with heavenly rays, and begging for the unity by which at last there may be one Fold and one Shepherd. (Jn. 10:16)

Every time a sinner is converted, every time a person seeks admission into the Church, every time a soul makes progress in virtue, it is Mary who influences him, who gives the grace and who brings him nearer to the Heart of Christ. For with her Son, it is her mission "to re-establish all things in Christ, that are in heaven and those that are on earth ... to make the two [Jews and gentiles, indeed, all human beings] into one man ... and to reconcile both to God in one body". The eminent preacher, Bossuet, cited Mary's activity in the Mystical Body of Christ: " ... her heart is in the hearts of all those who suffer in order to aid them to plead for mercy; in the wounds of all the injured to help them to beg for relief; in all charitable hearts to urge them to hasten to the alleviation, the support, the consolation of the needy and the afflicted; in all the

45

apostles in order to announce the Gospel; in all the martyrs in order to enable them to shed their blood; finally, in all the faithful, in order that they may observe the precepts, heed the counsels, and imitate the virtues". Such is the office, the function, and the operative love of Mary in the Church.

Pius XII promoted the work of Unity by his kindness to non-Catholics, by his affability in receiving people of other faiths, by his defense of the Jews during World War II, and by his various achievements for the Catholics of the Eastern rites. He founded the Damascenum for clergy of these rites, promulgated much of the Code of Canon Law for the East, sent messages of confidence and optimism to various celebrations and festivities in various parts of the world. He was especially concerned with Russia, for "On the conversion of Russia, now risen to the rank of a world power, depends not only the liberty and peace of the world, but also in great measure the conversion of other dissident peoples in Europe and in the East. And how profoundly would Protestantism be affected by it!" (Card. Agagianian)

In his letter for the Lourdes centenary (July 2, 1957) Pope Pius XII invited all the faithful to heed the advice of Our Lady, given to Bernadette: "Kindly come..." He renewed the intention of Pope Pius XI expressed for the Marian feasts of the Jubilee Year of 1933: "May the blind spirits... be illumined by the light of truth and justice, so that those who have gone astray in error may be brought back to the right path..." He asked specifically for the blessing of Unity: "May there be added to the prayers of the sick, of the humble, of all the pilgrims to Lourdes, that prayer to Mary that she may also turn her maternal gaze towards those who are still outside the limits of the only fold, the Church, so that they may come together in Unity. May she look upon those who seek and are thirsting for truth, and lead them to the source of living waters". This prayer and this hope has been amply taken up by his noble successor.

Pope John XXIII (1958 —)

Our Holy Father now gloriously reigning, Pope John XXIII, has shown himself most especially interested in the cause of Christian Unity, not only by the constant mention of unity in his addresses and less formal talks, but in a very special way, by calling a new general council of the Church. In the first address of his pontificate, he said: "And as we do the Western Church, we embrace with equal paternal affection the Eastern Church; we open our hearts and our arms to all those who are separated from the Apostolic See, where Peter himself lives in his successors until the 'end of the world' and fulfills the command given by Christ to bind and to loose all upon this earth and to shepherd the flock of the Lord. We ardently desire their return to the house of the Common Father, and we therefore repeat the words of the Divine Redeemer: "Holy Father, keep in thy name those whom thou hast given me, that they may be one even as we are.' In such a manner there shall be one sheepfold and one shepherd."

Again and again he has asked for prayers for Unity and for the success of the council. He has frequently spoken of Our Lady and the cause of reunion, as for example, before the Pentecost novena in May, 1959, he declared: "The most holy Mary is closely linked with the Church. She, in fact, 'preservering in prayer' together with the Apostles awaited in the cenacle the coming of the Holy Spirit who on the holy day of Pentecost gave the Church divine strength and made it possible for the Church to welcome to its bosom the multitude of the peoples." On another occasion, he urged the faithful to be fervent in love of Our

Lady, reminding them that "Through Mary to Jesus" is the way of Christian life. Again, when speaking of papal devotion to Our Lady, he said that "The house of the popes is the house of Mary," indicating the constant love of the Pontiffs for the Advocate and Protector of the Church, Our Blessed Lady. Early in 1960 the Holy Father made this plea: "Confide to Mary the great intentions of the Church—particularly that of the Ecumenical Council which is now the center of our preoccupations and for which we expect great things for the good of souls."

Love of Our Lady and prayer to her for the cause of Unity has been the theme of the pontiffs, particularly for the past century. It is an age-old refrain, recurring again and again in every age and among all peoples, and now with a greater urgency and significance than ever. May the faithful hearken to the voice of the present Pontiff in his efforts to promote devotion to Our Lady, and may they also realize that love for Mary and allegiance to the papacy are closely united, not only in the design of God, but even in the minds of those who are opposed to the Church. The papacy and the Blessed Virgin are the two great difficulties for nearly every person separated from the One Fold. Love for one will beget love for the other, and admiration for one will bring admiration for the other, so as to dispel difficulties and prepare the way for entrance into the one spiritual home of all men.

Three ❧ The Erection of the Barrier

"If you seek Jesus without Mary, you seek Him in vain".
—St. Bonaventure.

Within the compass of a few pages we cannot consider all or even many views of Our Lady held by those who profess to follow Christ but are separated from the Catholic Church. We seek to present a kind of cross-section of the attitudes and opinions which have given rise to the present-day situation. Our purpose in doing so is not to argue or dispute, but to present the position as fairly as possible. Ecumenism and Our Lady are closely related, as Fr. Burghardt has stated: "... It is surely significant that, save for the Catholic concept of the Church, the single theological issue which most effectively strangles the ecumenical dialogue is the Catholic vision of Mary. She is 'the wall' —if only because she is, for the Protestant, the visible symbol of Catholic idolatry: the Roman abandonment of scripture, of history, of Christ. Here too our dogmatic past scandalizes him, our dogmatic future baffles him. Divine maternity and perpetual virginity, an immaculate conception and a glorious assumption—these are already stones of stumbling. But the end is not yet: will Vatican Council II define, as part and parcel of God's public revelation, that the Virgin helped redeem the world? In this context it is not surprising to read an Anglican editorial which synthesizes non-Roman fears in a single sober sentence: 'Without apologizing for the Mariological vacuum so often found in Anglican thinking and devotion, it seems to us, at least, that there is an acute danger of the elevation of the Mother of God to a position out of accord with her status as a creature, as one of those whom her Son came to redeem.' "

The rejection of the Blessed Virgin Mary is not a religious phenomenon peculiar to the age in which we live. Nor did it begin as an aftermath of the Protestant Revolt or as a reaction against various apparitions within the last century. It has been part of the history of the Church to affirm the doctrine of Our Lady as revealed by God in every age and among all peoples. There have been exaggerations in writing and in devotion, but most difficulties of non-Catholics today stem, it seems, from premises that are incorrect and from conclusions that are unwarranted.

As early as 110 A.D. St. Ignatius, bishop of Antioch, warned Christians to be on their guard against the Docetists who considered the Incarnation a blasphemy. "Stop your ears," he said, "when anyone speaks to you that stands apart from Jesus Christ, from David's scion and Mary's Son, who was really born and ate and drank, was really persecuted by Pontius Pilate, really crucified and died . . . who really rose from the dead . . ."

Gnosticism tried to separate Christ from His Mother by denying His sacred humanity. Cerinthus said Jesus was the Son of Mary and Joseph, conceived and born as any other child. Marcion said that Jesus was a full-grown man, without a human mother. Faustus and the Manichees tried to deny the virginity of Mary and say that Jesus came from the earth. St. Augustine vented his scorn on such an opinion in this fashion: "Dare you compare the holiness of that

50

chaste virgin's womb with any piece of ground where trees and plants grow? Do you pretend to look with abhorrence upon a pure Virgin while you do not shrink from believing that Jesus is produced in gardens watered by the filthy drains of a city?"

The Arians in the fourth century denied that Mary was the Mother of God; for them she was only the Mother of Christ. Athanasius spoke the Catholic doctrine when he cried: "That Word was born of the Father from above . . . and eternally, the very same in time and here below is born of Mary, the Virgin Mother of God." St. Gregory of Naziansenum stated that the title *Theotokos* was not only a test of orthodoxy, but a requirement for eternal salvation. "If anyone does not accept holy Mary as Mother of God, he is cut off from the Deity."

The Patriarch, John of Antioch, a friend of Nestorius, had urged him "not to refuse unhesitatingly to call the Holy Virgin the Mother of God . . . For if we do not accept what is implied by this name, then we must inevitably deceive ourselves in many things, and fall into special danger regarding the ineffable work of the Redemption by the Incarnate Son of God. For if we dismiss this name and all that it means, we shall very quickly come to deny that the author of our glorious redemption was God, and that the Word emptied Himself, taking the form of a servant, thus showing us the immeasurable greatness of His love." History bears out how well-founded was the anxiety of the patriarch for his friend.

In 431 the Council of Ephesus proclaimed the Divine Motherhood of Our Lady. At once the faithful followed the instincts of their minds and hearts and placed icons of Mary near those of her Son; they kept feasts in her honor, and both the East and West incorporated a beautiful new phrase that would give her the primacy next to her Son: " . . . in the first place, the memory of the glorious and

51

ever Virgin Mary, Mother of God and of our Lord Jesus Christ." Following the joyful era of Ephesus, new praises arose in her honor. St. Proclus of Constantinople called Mary the "only bridge of God to men." Theodotus of Ancyre hailed her as "more glorious than paradise." St. Cyril of Alexandria could say: "Through you, O Mary, the apostles preached salvation to the nations . . . through you the precious cross is honored and adored throughout the world; through you every person who was held by the error of idolatry is led back to recognize the truth; through you the faithful have come to holy baptism and churches have been founded in every nation."

St. Cyril, the leading spirit at Ephesus, thus pointed to Mary's influence in the spread of the gospel and in the extension of God's kingdom on earth. Mary leads back those who have fallen away through apostasy or indifference; she gives spiritual life to new members of the Church. She is the Mother of the world.

In one of his paeans of praise, this doctor cried out: "Hail from us, Mary . . . the sceptre of orthodoxy!" The centuries have only confirmed the validity of this statement, for the acceptance or rejection of Our Lady has meant the acceptance or rejection of Christ and all revealed teaching. Cardinal Newman could write, fourteen hundred years later, after the onslaughts upon Our Lady and three hundred years of Protestant defection: "The Church and Satan agreed in this, that Son and Mother went together; and the experience of three centuries has confirmed their testimony, for Catholics who have honored the Mother, still worship the Son, while Protestants who now have ceased to confess the Son, began then by scoffing at the Mother."

Following the patristic period there was no major attack on Our Lady. The papacy was in distress at times, and there was little development in the intellectual and spiritual life until the Middle Ages, when saints and doctors consecrated the gifts of their minds and hearts to the all-glorious Queen of heaven. The medieval period gave rise to a clarification of one of the most attractive of all teachings about Mary, the Immaculate Conception. Some of the greatest preachers in the history of the Church were conspicuous for their intense love of the Mother of God, such as St. Anthony of Padua, St. Bernardine of Siena, St. John Capistran, St. Peter Verona, St. Antonine of Florence and St. Vincent Ferrer.

Then came the blight of the sixteenth century in England, Germany, France, the Low Countries and Scandinavia. The Church reeled under the blow, but she did not fall. From confusion and persecution there came new strength to Catholics and new honors for Our Lady. At Bourgillon, Switzerland, the faithful rallied to her shrine, begging her help to ward off dangers in the canton of Fribourg. For months Catholics went in pilgrimage to her shrine, and when the danger passed they gratefully inscribed at the base of the Statue: "Our Lady of Bourgillon, Defender of the Faith." St. Peter Canisius frequently visited this holy place, for Mary is the defender of the faith not only for a Swiss canton, but for the entire world.

In 1520 the Minister General of the Franciscan Order, Francis Licheto, ordered every friary to prepare special preachers against Lutheranism. In 1521 the General Chapter of Capri ordered prayers to the Mother of God; at the end of each hour of the office were added the words: "Rejoice and be glad, O Virgin Mary, because thou alone has destroyed all heresies through the world." The friars prayed for resistance even to the shedding of their blood, and often their prayers were answered with a soldier's sword or a hangman's noose. Such heroism was demonstrated also by other religious communities and by the faithful diocesan clergy.

In the beginning, the reformers did not reject Our

Lady. Martin Luther was attracted by the Magnificat of Mary and wrote a long commentary upon it. In the preface he wrote: "May the same tender Mother of God obtain for me the spirit to interpret her son usefully and practically ...that we may sing and chant this *Magnificat* eternally in the life to come. So help us God. Amen." In conclusion, he expressed the hope that a correct understanding of the Magnificat "may not only illumine and teach, but burn and live in body and soul; may Christ grant us this by the intercession and assistance of His dear Mother Mary. Amen." It should be noted, however, that at the same time he wrote his words of praise of Our Lady, he also attacked the pope, thus showing the contradictory positions which he had already espoused. Later on, he repudiated the traditional devotion to the Mother of God, although he seems to have believed in the Immaculate Conception and the Assumption until his death. After 1522, he said she held no special place in God's plan for the salvation of the world, that her prayers were not more than those of others, that the *Salve Regina* was "a great blasphemy against God."

The first of the confessional writings, the Augsburg Confession of 1530, drawn up by Melancthon with Luther's approval, held that "the Word, that is, the Son of God, assumed a human nature in the womb of the Blessed Virgin Mary, with the result that the two natures, the human and the divine, (are) inseparably united in the unity of the person, one Christ, truly God and truly man, born of the Virgin Mary." In the last of the confessional writings, the Formula of Concord of 1579, the expression was fuller: "By reason of this hypostatic union and the communion of natures, Mary, that Virgin most worthy of praise, brought forth not only a man but such a man as is truly the Son of the Most High God, as the archangel Gabriel bears witness. He, the Son of God, showed forth His Majesty as well in that he was born of a virgin, her virginity inviolate.

And thus she is truly *Theotokos,* and yet remained a virgin." Luther acknowledged that veneration of Our Lady "is inscribed in the very depths of the human heart." He said that men should invoke her "in order that God for her sake, will give and bring to accomplishment that which we ask." He defended the Divine Maternity against Nestorius and accepted the Immaculate Conception. In general, care was taken not to make radical and sudden changes in regard to Our Lady. This in itself was an indication of steadfast attachment to the Marian devotion. In the document concerned with the discipline of churches, the *Ecclesiastical Constitution,* there was cited the need of retaining the feasts of Our Lady which are also feasts of Our Lord, such as the Annunciation, the Purification and Visitation. In the city statutes of Gorlitz, three feasts were to be celebrated: the Nativity, the Assumption and the Conception of Mary, though by 1569 some cities had ceased to keep these festivals.

Later Lutherans and other Protestants rejected the traditional devotion to the Mother of God. But through the centuries, two feasts of Our Lady were always celebrated in most sections of Germany, the Annunciation and the Assumption. Zwingli, Knox, and Calvin did not begin their departure from the Church by demeaning Our Lady. In fact, their followers have, on the whole, shunned Our Lady much more than did their leaders. Cramner and Elizabeth finished the sad work begun in England, though Henry VIII had asked for Masses and for prayers to Our Lady for the repose of his soul. It was necessary to promulgate laws in Prussia to prevent Lutherans from celebrating the feasts of the Blessed Virgin.

Catholics have been accused of worshipping Our Lady, in the sense of giving her adoration due to God alone. They have been called "Mariolatrists," who place the Blessed Virgin in the position of Almighty God. The accusation is false, as any book on Catholic teaching will show, but the charge has been made over and over again. Our Lady's virginity has been called "superstitious and degrading."

Non-Catholic leaders of the sixteenth century accepted the teaching on the Immaculate Conception, for the most part. But not so their followers. It came to be called a myth, and Karl von Hase said that it may well evolve "into the destructive power of the Christian form of worship which ... belongs to a past period of history." Pusey wrote against it in the last century and many Anglican divines in this age, but surely not all of them. A more moderate view was that of Dr. J. Hall, who said: "Though the doctrine of the Immaculate Conception has been defined by papal authority, it is not an ancient nor generally admitted belief. Moreover, one cannot find convincing testimony proving it." But there are above one thousand clergymen of the Anglican "high church" who profess belief in the Immaculate Conception.

Von Hase declared that the future would be dark for the Church after the proclamation of the Immaculate Conception. Actually, it was the beginning of a new era. He was indeed correct when he said that "Protestant nations ... have shown coldness for the Mother of Our Lord." But he veered back to a traditional concept when he added: "Nevertheless, we cannot deny that Jesus Christ is also honored in His Mother, and we must consider her like a treasure, not only in her scriptural simplicity, but also in her artistic glorification." It was a case of respect for her rather than love which made James Cooper ask himself if such an attitude actually led to a more vivid faith in Christ, and if it encouraged the Christian ideal of purity, generosity, and holiness.

There are other indications of a stir within non-Catholic circles at the present time. As the prominent Anglican clergyman, Dr. E. L. Mascall of Oxford has said: "Christianity without Mary is a monstrosity," and many converts to the Church from Anglicanism have had a deep devotion to the Mother of God. Douglas Hyde and others began their journey to the Church through devotion to the Mother of God.

Protestants fear that Mary takes the place of Christ. She is the "mediator between man and God for millions of Catholics everywhere." Sometimes the charge is even made that the development of devotion to Our Lady had its origin as a transfer from some pagan worship. "Devotion to Mary has progressed from this obscure heresy in the fourth century to the decision of the Roman Pope that it is necessary to salvation for a Christian to believe her to have been free of original sin even from the first moment of her Conception." (James Hastings Nichols)

Dr. Thompson has tried to popularize Jung's theory of the "collective consciousness" as applied to the veneration of Our Lady, and argued that there was a gradual relapse into polytheistic practices and an expression of the feminine element in religions of the Near East, even though the earliest Christian communities remained loyal to the mono-theistic concept of religion. "Opposed to the endeavor to form a unity there stands a still strong endeavor to create again and again a multiplicity, so that even in the so-called monotheistic religions, as Christianity for example, the poly-theistic tendency is irrepressible. The Deity is divided into three parts at least, to which is added the feminine deity of Mary and the numerous company of lesser gods, the angels and saints respectively."

All of which, to the Catholic, is a jumble of unfounded assumptions and assertions. Any manual of Catholics teaching makes clear that there is but one God, that Our Lady is a creature, greatly exalted, but still a creature, and that the angels and saints are in no sense to be called "lesser gods." It is sometimes difficult to be patient with those who make assertions through gross misunderstanding.

Protestant opposition to Our Lady has reached a point of charging Catholics with Mariolotry, and of other excesses in devotion to the Mother of God. Catholics do not adore the Blessed Virgin; adoration is for God alone. They recognize Our Lady, however glorious and influential with God she may be, is still a creature, however greatly endowed. Archbishop Geoffrey Fischer, formerly of Canterbury, Bishop Henry Knox Sherrill of New York City and other Anglican prelates assailed the definition of the Assumption of Our Lady in 1950. Some stated that it widened the breach between the Catholic Church and non-Catholics. John Frederick Olson in *Christian Century* (1950, vol. 67, col. 1, 161) denounced the definition of the Assumption as a formidable obstacle to the ecumenical movement and as an underscoring of the "Roman Catholic rejection of scripture as containing all the truths necessary for salvation and as the sole rule of faith and action."

Another Episcopalian clergyman stated at the time that "It seems to me that the depths of theological degradation must surely be reached in the very act of using the Mother of Jesus to divide the one, holy, Catholic and apostolic Church which He founded." It is a curious statement that Mary divides the Church, which cannot be divided; her only interest is to glorify God and bring men to salvation. A mother unites her children through the bonds of confidence and love.

The famous and popular Swiss theologian, Karl Barth, has often written against Marian theology. For him "The content of the biblical attestation of revelation does not give us any cause to acknowledge that the person of Mary in the event of revelation possesses relatively even such an independent and emphatic position as to render it necessary or justifiable to make it the objection of a theological doctrine. Mariology is an excrescence, i.e., a diseased construct of theological thought. Excrescences must be exised."

A modern non-Catholic writer states that "in the Roman Catholic Church great prominence is given to Mary every day of the year." (Schaff, *Primer on Roman Catholicism for Protestants*) He further states that Protestants hear about Our Lady only twice in the year—at Christmas and at Easter. "Protestants think of Mary as the ideal Mother but never the 'Mother of God'. They also think of the apparitions, miracles and special blessings from Mary as bordering on superstition. For some "Mary is an ecclesiastical fiction which has grown with the centuries until it was turned into a dogma by the arbitrary utterances of Pius IX, that she was born without sin. Mariology may have its historical significance during the age of chivalry in exalting womanly purity but the scriptures have no syllable to justify it. . . . Sinners do not need Mary's mediation to reach their Saviour and then him to reach God . . ."

The published correspondence between Archbishop Gerald P. O'Hara of Savannah, Ga., and the Baptist Minister, Rev. Dick Houston Hall, Jr., was concerned in part with the position of Our Lady in Catholic teaching and devotion. Among the eight doctrines of which the clergyman asked for an explanation were three points on Our Lady: The Immaculate Conception, prayer to Mary, and her Assumption into heaven. His chief objection seemed to be that Our Lady replaces Christ and that she performs functions that are His. It was not a new charge, of course, but it showed that the old objections are still being cited. The Archbishop wrote: "May I say how baffling it is to Catholics to find that sincere followers of Christ, such as yourselves, do not in fact speak more often of Mary and pay more honor to her? We understand indeed that you may not be fully convinced of the doctrines we teach concerning her but we find it hard to understand how your reverences to the Mother of Christ should so often be lacking in any kind of affection for her."

The prelate stated very briefly that "Mary's intercession is necessary only in the measure that Christ has willed it. It is no challenge to His unique, universal mediation that He should have appointed an Almoner of all his graces."

And so the difficulty continues. In the introduction to this book, we referred to the incident in South Africa in 1958 when a stamp for anti-tuberculosis seals was withdrawn because it was considered offensive to the Dutch Reformed Church. But someone showed an official Bible of this religious group, published in 1714, which showed the Madonna and Child with halos. A further reaction to the incident was the remark of the Anglican bishop of Johannesburg, who was taken back by the attacks on the stamp of the Madonna and Child. "I am shocked," he stated, "not only by the attack on the Roman Catholic Church but by the fact that the protest contains an unwarranted assumption that only Roman Catholics revere the Mother of Jesus."

The rejection by the Orthodox groups takes a different form than the objections of the Protestants. Generally speaking, Protestants reject devotion to Our Lady completely, while the separated brethren of the East are intensely devoted to her; in some instances, far more than Catholics. But the Orthodox peoples reject the definitions of "The Bishop of Rome," as they call the Pope, because they do not accept his supremacy. They are not opposed to the exaltation of our Lady.

It is also a sad fact that the definition of the Assumption meant a rejection of the teaching, on many sides, by the Orthodox. It was somewhat similar to the failure of belief in the East in the Immaculate Conception of Our Lady after it was defined in 1854 by Pope Pius IX.

Ildephone Cardinal Schuster of Milan has commented

thus on the matter: "The Eastern Christians among whom the most ancient and most explicit testimonies for the Immaculate Conception were to be found, declared themselves opposed to the dogma because it had been promulgated by the 'Bishop of ancient Rome', whom they viewed with unfriendly eyes and they accused the papal party of introducing an innovation. Yet, as far back as the end of the seventeenth century the Jesuit, Fr. Besson, after having pointed out by means of 200 passages drawn from their liturgies the perfect agreement of the early Eastern fathers with the Latin doctors concerning the Immaculate Conception, obtained from them a definite declaration written and signed by three patriarchs and an archimandrite."

Fr. Joseph Besson, S.J. quoted this statement from the head of the Syrian Church: "I, Ignatius Andrew, unworthy Antiochene patriarch of Syria, confirm this orthodox opinion which Fr. Joseph (Besson) of the Society of Jesus has explained, that the most holy and pure Virgin Mary was always free from and immune from original sin, as the venerable Fathers, the teachers of the Eastern Church, have taught."

The repudiation of the Immaculate Conception was not due to a rejection of Our Lady but to a mistrust of the Pope. This was also true, it would seem, in regard to the definition of the Assumption. But other prominent theologians such as T. G. Spassky, George Florovsky, and Sergius Bulgakov, have asserted that the Assumption is a necessary compliment to Our Lady's dignity as Mother of God. Dr. Spassky declared that "The consonance between the Orthodox and the Catholic concept of the Assumption of the Mother of God into heaven also places in relief a fundamental agreement on Marian doctrine."

Thus, the barrier or the chasm of disunity continues. The obstacles are many and complex and increased over the centuries. But not all the words from the Protestant

61

brethren are those of condemnation. There are some whose praise is eloquent and valuable.

An Evangelical pastor in Germany, Johann Lortzing, has written this deeply touching interpretation of the Sistine Madonna which hangs in the Dresden Art Gallery in a special room. Perhaps it echoes the sentiments of more people than we know. He stated that a person "must actually feel startled at first glance at the almost threatening attitude of the Blessed Virgin." Then he went on with his meditation. "It is as though she wished to say: 'Back, back all of you who wish to take Him from me, the Son of God and my Son. If you cruelly tear Him from me, in time you will lose Him. The Child will allow no one to carry him but His Mother. See how proudly, how securely He rests upon my protecting arm. He who parts from me will in time part from my Child; he who denies the Mother will eventually deny the Son. You must decide whether you will have me with Him or renounce both of us. And if you return to the Mother, you also find the Son again. He has been entrusted to me! No one can tear Him from me and go unpunished; none can wholly possess Him who does not accept Mother and Son. It is a delusion to say that I supplant my Son or put Him in the shade. I am His guardian; I am His Protectress; I show Him to the world; I bear Him in my arms so that all the world may see Him, know Him, and love Him.'"

Max Jungnickel, also in Germany, has tenderly promised to restore veneration to Our Lady. "We miss Mother Mary. We must fetch her back. She will blossom forth like a rose from the cold stone of our churches. We shall adorn her with flowers from the fields and branches from the woods to celebrate her home-coming. And we will pray and sing to her." But not many of his co-religionists would share his sentiments.

More recently we have the words of a Lutheran in

January, 1956, regarding the apparitions of Mary during the past century and her mediation in the lives of men. It was an unusual document, a plea for an understanding of Fatima, Lourdes, and La Salette. It stated that either Fatima is a tremendous fraud in which the Catholic Church is gravely in error, or it is true and meant "for the whole of Christianity, for the whole world. Today, when the very existence or non-existence of Christianity in different nations is at stake, should we not be failing our duty if we were to shut our ears to the Voice of God Who speaks to the world through the mediation of Mary, simply because that Voice has come to us through the Catholic Church?"

The writer then called upon Christians to open their hearts to these appeals of Our Lady and to examine them, lest they run the risk "of rejecting the saving hand of God." Would that more non-Catholics would wish to consider Our Lady's role in the history of the world and in the salvation of mankind.

This brief survey only confirms what Cardinal Ottaviani declared at the Marian Congress held at Lourdes in September, 1958: "It is an unchanging law wherever the devotion to the Mother is retained, the Son has remained present with her, and His Vicar has continued to be the guarantee of the unity of His Mystical Body. Protestantism left no place for Mary. For, in repudiating the altar of the Son, it repudiated the shrine of the Mother at the same time. In refusing obedience to the Vicar of Jesus Christ, the Protestants have scattered like sheep who fail to hear the voice of the shepherds. In vain will they struggle to find unity again apart from Jesus present in the Eucharist, and apart from Our Lady and the Pope."

And so the holy Mother of God and the Mother of all men is so vitally important for the apostolate of Christian reunion. Our Lady is the means selected by God to unite all her children in the one Church. She does not impede or hinder; she facilitates and promotes the work of Christian Unity. It is the role of a mother to unite her children—and who better than Mary can bring together all the peoples of the world into the only fold, the one family of her beloved Son?

Four ❧ Our Lady and Ecumenism

> "Jesu that dost in Mary dwell
> Be in thy servants' hearts as well . . .
> —G. M. Hopkins, S.J.

In the quiet summer of 1910, leaders of the Protestant world convened in Edinburgh, Scotland, for the World Missionary Conference. It was the culmination and development of many similar meetings during the 19th century, and it marked the beginning of the modern ecumenical movement.

During the half century since the Edinburgh meeting, additional efforts have been made by non-Catholics of nearly every persuasion. The assemblies of the World Council of Churches, in Amsterdam (1948) and in Evanston (1954), were large-scale efforts directed towards reunion. In September, 1961, the Pan-Orthodox meeting was held at the Island of Rhodes, the first gathering in more than a thousand years. In November, 1961, the third assembly of the World Council of Churches met in New Delhi, India. All over the world there is an increased desire for unity among those who are separated from the Catholic Church.

The desire for unity on the part of our separated

brethren has brought them to a closer study of the Catholic position. It has made them aware of Catholic teaching, not only on the Church, but also and especially on the Blessed Virgin Mary. But they view Our Lady, not as the great means of effecting unity, but as an obstacle of staggering proportions. The stumbling block is not only the primacy and infallibility of the Roman Pontiff, but the Virgin Maid of Nazareth, the Mother of Christ.

Indeed, as Fr. Thomas Clarke, S.J., has stated:

> When Catholics and Protestants agree to disagree, the name of Mary is almost sure to be mentioned. Today, in many quarters, Simeon's prophecy is being verified with a peculiar twist: She is the sign of contradiction, the rock of scandal—and this not only for cynical unbelievers, who for a century have tried to sneer Lourdes out of existence, but for devout Christians, who profess the faith of Nicea and Chalcedon. It is truly ironic that the very things which bring Catholics *ad Jesum per Mariam*—the processions of Lourdes and Fatima, the papal definition of the Assumption—have become for many Protestants symbols of Rome's apostasy from the unique Mediator, Jesus Christ.

Without prejudice to Protestant good faith, we wish to review some of their assertions about Our Lady in relation to the question of Christian Unity.

Hans Rudei Weber was the only Protestant among the two thousand Catholics who attended the World Congress of the Lay Apostolate in Rome in October, 1957. He found much of the Congress praiseworthy and inspiring; he was delighted that he could be present. But for him the emphasis given to the place of the Mother of God in the apostolate presented grave problems. He noted that Pope Pius XII confided all forms of the lay apostolate "to Mary, the glorious and mighty Queen of Heaven". But these tributes meant, in his mind, a deification of her, and the placing of all apostolic works under her banner "make any fruitful conversation and collaboration . . . increasingly difficult".

Going back some years to other meetings dealing with unity, we find other Marian sidelights. In 1927, at the First World Conference on Faith and Order, in Lausanne, Prof. Sergius Bulganov, dean of the Orthodox Theological Institute of Paris, introduced a consideration of Our Lady when the question under discussion was the Christian norm of Faith. He said:

> Holiness—the holiness of the manhood of Christ, actualized by the communion of saints—is the goal and essence of the Church's life. But we cannot separate the humanity of Our Lord from that of His Mother, the unspotted *Theotokos*. She is the head of mankind in the Church; Mother and Bride of the Lamb, she is joined with all the saints and angels in the worship and life of the Church. Others may not feel drawn, as I do, to name her in prayer. Yet, as we draw together toward doctrinal reunion, it may be that we are coming potentially nearer even in her regard.

The chairman of the meeting, Dr. A. E. Garvie (Congregationalist), stopped the speaker and called attention to his departure from the subject under discussion. But the professor refused to accept the ruling and renewed his plea for the recognition of Mariology as a doctrinal problem of vital importance in the ecumenical movement. His persistence was crowned with some success, for the communion of saints was included in the agenda of the second Faith and Order Conference held in Edinburgh in 1937. On this occasion an Orthodox spokesman said that the question of the communion of saints, of which the recognition of the

67

Blessed Virgin Mary is a part, deserves a high place on the agenda of Christian Unity.

In recent years, non-Catholic theologians have written on Our Lady, notably Pastor Charles Brutsch and Pastor Jean de Saussure in France, and Dr. Hans Asmussen and Prof. Wilhelm Stahlin in Germany. They do not accept the full Catholic belief on Our Lady, but they seem to recognize the challenge that she presents to sincere theologians. Professor Maury of Paris affirmed that "the doctrine of Mary and the cult of the Virgin seems to me to pose with increasing precision and with an unmistakable clarity the real problem of our relations with the Roman Church".

Karl Barth, in his *Church Dogmatics,* rejects completely the Catholic doctrine on Our Lady as taught by Scheeben and other leading Catholic theologians. He calls it "that heresy of the Roman Catholic Church which makes all her other heresies understandable". Moreover, he says "that Church which renders worship to Mary is bound to conceive of herself as she actually did at the Vatican Council". In reality, he is paying tribute to the coherence and consistency of Catholic doctrine, which is one confirmatory evidence of its truth. On the other hand, he accepts the title "Mother of God" as defined at the Council of Ephesus in 431, and defends the doctrine of the virgin birth. Holding, as he does, to the doctrine of the Divine Maternity, it is strange that he rejects its implications, for all the prerogatives of Mary flow from it as from a fountainhead. The Italian Waldensian, Giovanni Miegge, acknowledges in his work, *The Virgin Mary,* that Our Lady is the Mother of God, but he considers Mariology "a slap at Catholic Unity".

In 1951 the Commission on Faith and Order published its *Report on Ways of Worship.* In the introduction it said: "It is in our approach to one another in the way of worship that our differences about the Virgin Mary are most clearly exposed. We may find it comparatively easy to discuss the reverence due her, or to analyze the psychological backgrounds of our different practices; it is quite another thing to be put in the attitude of decision by being asked to join in prayer to her." Thus, while they are quite willing to discuss Our Lady, they are not willing to pray to her. The statement was signed by the officers of the commission: G. van der Leeuw, Hans Asmussen and Wiebe Vos.

About one-third of the report was devoted to Mariology. Fr. Conrad Pepler, O.P., made a contribution for the Catholic concept; Prof. Vladimir Lossky for the Orthodox, Rev. T. M. Parker for the Anglicans and Max Thurian of the French Reformed Church for the Calvinist position. On the first page of his paper Max Thurian made this provocative charge: "The doctrine and the veneration of Mary in the Roman Church creates extreme difficulties for ecumenical thought . . . one can see no way through the problem posed by Mariology and the veneration of the Blessed Virgin in the Church". And he stated his thesis once more: "Catholic Mariology poses the most agonizing problem for ecumenical thought".

But before he concluded his paper, M. Thurian referred to the spiritual power of Our Lady in the cause of reunion as the head of the communion of saints: "The great litany of the saints is the most moving and strongest ecumenical prayer. And Mary is present at the head of this general assumbly of the Church and of the first-born whose names are written in heaven". We think, however, that he holds more strongly to his first statement.

Reinhold Niebuhr echoed similar negative sentiments when Pope Pius XII issued the call for a Marian Year in 1954. "Any lingering envy," he commented, "which many of us have had for the Roman Catholic unity was recently dispelled by the constant effort of the Church to exalt the Virgin Mary until she has become a virtual replacement of the Holy Spirit in the Trinity." In a special article in *The*

Atlantic (Aug. 1962) Dr. Niebuhr made the same criticism: "Another basic religious cause of tension is the increased Mariolotry of modern Catholicism. Building on Catholic piety with roots preceding even the mediaeval period, the Church, for some mysterious reason, has chosen to widen the breach between it and modern culture. In a series of dogmas promulgated in the later nineteenth century and extending into this very century, it virtually lifted the Virgin Mary into the Godhead (some say into the Trinity) replacing the less historical Holy Spirit." For us the statement is quite confused and very misleading. It seems strange that a clergyman of his stature should still accuse Catholics of "adoring" Our Lady, even if he should consider Marian piety as a cause of tension and disunity. Similarly, the General Assembly of Presbyterians meeting in Los Angeles in 1955 said that the Catholic emphasis on Our Lady has widened the breach between Catholics and all other Christian denominations.

Dr. John Mackay, president of Princeton Theological Seminary, was the author of the document. It was a complete denunciation of the Marian Year and of Catholic devotion to the Mother of God. "In the celebration of that year," he said, "the progressive trend to exalt the figure of the Virgin Mother to the office of an associate partner in the work of Redemption reaches its culminating climax. Mary of Nazareth has become Co-Redemptrix with her Son." Of course, Catholics do hold that Our Lady shared in the mystery of Calvary in such a close and unique way as to be Reparatrix of a fallen world. The terms and the titles applied to Our Lady originated with the fathers of the Church centuries ago.

Besides attacking the Immaculate Conception, the Assumption, and various modern titles for Our Lady, he ridiculed the apparitions of the Blessed Virgin at Fatima.

Then he made sweeping assertions against Our Lady and the Church. We doubt that he means his statement that "Nothing is more distasteful than to subject to unfavorable analysis developments which occur in another Christian communion". He rather seems to delight in it.

Without giving undue prominence to the unwarranted charges (made, we feel, because he does not fully understand Catholic teaching on Our Lady), we may cite some of the issues raised. Obviously, he rejects the historical evidence for the miraculous phenomena at Fatima (and, we presume, any other apparition): "A deep gulf exists between the Virgin of Nazareth and the Virgin of Fatima ... developed Mariology of our time is the response to a craving which has been keenly felt in Roman Catholic circles". The Marian cult today fills a vacuum created in the Church by the Council of Trent. She is "the incarnation of the Holy Ghost, the executive director of the Trinity". Dr. Mackay surely can find no shred of evidence in any papal document to give rise to such a gratuitous statement.

He went on: "The development of the Marian cult has widened the breach between the Roman Catholic Church and all other Christian communions. In the figure of the Virgin, the Church of Rome has created a semi-divine female being, who becomes the virtual head of the Church." Writings of this kind are serious obstacles to working for reunion. But he continued his gratuitous remarks:

> The Marian cult continues a challenge to all Evangelical Christians. The glory of Christ's headship in His Church, his undying concern for members of His Body and all human beings, is both tarnished and challenged by the new status accorded to the Virgin.

It is not surprising then that Dr. Mackay would then write the preface for the book by G. Meigge, a Waldensian,

71

on our Lady. In his brief remarks he declared that the question of Mary "poses a crucial problem for contemporary Christianity". He called her "the executive director of the Deity, the ultimate mediator of God's grace to men".

Waldo Smith, who translated the work, wrote the foreword: "To the Protestant Christian, the cult of Mary is disquieting and perplexing. Mary in Roman Catholic devotion is the preferred object of devotion. Mary has eclipsed her Son. There has been another eclipse, too. The devotion to Mary, in its operation, hides and virtually negates the warmest and most profound truth in Jesus' teaching—the fatherhood of God."

But even more specific was the charge that Mariology is the great barrier for those outside the Church. "A regrettable side to the current Mariology is its injury to Christian unity. It is widening the rift between the Roman and the Greek Catholic Churches. It makes an ever wider separation between Roman Catholics and Protestants . . . But Marian devotion has gone to lengths in belief and observance that the Protestant faith can never accept. Its promotors are carrying the Roman Catholic Church away from Christian unity faster than Protestants can approach it. Their policy is enlarging the doctrinal schism of Christendom." (Canon Geo. Smith)

These statements only corroborate the observation of a comparison made between Catholics and Protestants some years ago by William Brown: "There is no point which presents a greater obstacle to the Protestant, none which is more essential to understand, if we wish to penetrate the essence of Catholic piety . . . At no point is the tension more acute than in the attitude taken towards Mary . . . which to Protestants, however explained and restricted, has seemed blasphemous and its rejection a necessary condition of maintaining the unique distinction and final supremacy of Jesus".

While some Anglican prelates denounced the Catholic Church when the Assumption was defined, a number of the clergy and people were high in praise of Mary's exaltation. There are other currents of Marian devotion among members of the Protestant Episcopal Church. For the book of Common Prayer, some have substituted the American Missal with many pro-Marian features. The calendar has been enlarged to include such feasts as Our Lady of Mount Carmel, Our Lady of Clemency, Our Lady of Perpetual Help, Our Lady of Guadalupe, Our Lady of the Rosary, the Seven Sorrows, the Holy Name of Mary and the Expectation. These indications point to a deepening of Marian piety which will surely lead some of its members to the Catholic Church. The Scottish and the South African prayer books stress the merits and intercession of Our Lady, and the former commemorates the appearance of Christ to His Mother after the Resurrection. Dr. Bernard I. Bell, St. James Church, Chicago, has spoken thus: "Next to the Lord Jesus Himself, it is Mary, the Mother of Jesus, who has most fully understood the power of the Holy Spirit, who has known what it means, inspired by Him to be a co-worker with God . . . In all history there is no human being who has had a larger influence for social righteousness than blessed Mary . . . Never will a human being be of use worth mentioning, toward the building of a better world, until God the Holy Spirit . . . abides in us as He abides in Mary." (*Altar and the World*, New York: Harper, 1944, 90).

Even the profligate poet, Lord Byron, could appreciate the place of Our Lady. He wrote of her in these lines describing the ruins of Newstead Abbey:

But in a high niche, alone, but crown'd
　The Virgin Mother of the God-born child,
With her Son in her blessed arms, look'd 'round,

73

Spared by some change when all beside
was spoil'd;
She made the earth below seem holy ground.

In 1857, Pusey wrote his charges against Our Lady
which brought forth a defense from the renowned Newman, for her presence had marked his entire life. In his
sermon notes of 1851, he wrote: "... thirty years this year
since I was brought under the shadow of Our Lady, whom
I ever wished to love more and more". And to a friend
he said: "My college was St. Mary's and my church; when
I went to Littlemore there was Our Blessed Lady waiting
for me." She waited for him in the zeal and love of Fr.
Dominic Barberi, C.P., who received the great luminary of
England into the Church of his ancestors in 1845. When
Newman wrote in defense of the Church and Our Lady in
The Difficulties of Anglicans in answer to the charges of
Pusey, he stated (on the eve of the Immaculate Concep-
tion, 1865):

And now when I could wish to proceed, she seems
to stop all controversy, for the feast of her Immaculate Conception is upon us; and close upon its Octave
which is kept with special solemnities in the churches
of this town, come the great Antiphons, the heralds of
Christmas. That joyful season, joyful for all of us, while
it centers in Him who then came to earth, also brings
before us in peculiar prominence that Virgin Mother
who bore and nursed Him. She is not in the background as at Easter-tide, but she brings Him to us in
her arms. Two great festivals dedicated to her honor,
tomorrow's and the Purification, mark out and keep the
ground like the towers of David, open the way to and
fro, from the high holiday season of the Prince of Peace.
And all along it, her image is upon it, such as

we see it in the typical representations of the catacombs. May the sacred influence of this tide *bring us together in unity!* May it destroy all bitterness on your side and ours! May it quench all jealous, sour, proud, fierce antagonism on our side; and dissipate all captious, carping, fastidious refinements of reasoning on yours! May that bright and gentle Lady, the Blessed Virgin Mary, overcome you with her sweetness and revenge herself upon her foes by interceding effectually for their conversion.

Such, too, is our prayer.

Our Blessed Lady is "Holy Mary meek and mild", the Mother "of fair love and holy hope". But she is also "the great sign appeared in heaven, a woman clothed with the sun". She is the great power of heaven and the feared enemy of Hell. She is "more powerful than an army in battle array" as the Church likes to sing of her. Her love is effective for men by the will of Him who gave her to men. "It is her prayers that avail and her prayers are effectual by the will of Him who is our all in all. Nor need she hear us by any innate power or any personal gift; but by His manifestation to her of the prayers which we make to her. When Moses was on the mount, the Almighty told him of the idolatry of his people at the foot of it, in order that he might intercede for them; and thus, it is the Divine Presence which is the intermediating Power by which we reach her and she reaches us." (Cardinal Newman).

The Protestant charge of Rome's apostasy from Christ, the one Mediator, seems to derive from a mistaken concept of Catholic theology and devotion. They consider the cooperation of any creature—not excluding Mary—in the plan of salvation and sanctification not as a parallel action with God, undertaken jointly, but rather a vertical cooperation, so that the creature serves God's purpose and is subordinated to Him. Catholic teaching holds that all grace comes from Christ and all mediation is in Him alone, though exercised through the ministry of the Church in some way and through the intercession of Our Lady.

The deep devotion of the Eastern Orthodox to Our Lady furnishes hope for their reunion with the Holy See. And there are some hopeful signs among other separated brethren, too. Dr. Hans Asmussen has said that "Catholics with their devotion to the Virgin have a Christology that is more profound than that of Protestants, who wish to venerate Christ alone". Another clergyman told Fr. Charles Boyer, S.J., in Rome: "We are discovering devotion to the Blessed Virgin and it is truly enriching us." There is hope from the resolution of the World Lutheran Federation's meeting in Minneapolis in 1957, which went on record as advocating a study of the Catholic theological system. In Darmstadt, Germany, there is a thriving community known as the Evangelical Sisterhood of St. Mary, whose principal aim is to pray for reunion. Their activities are carried out under the special invocation of the Blessed Virgin.

The American Lutheran theologian, Dr. Jaroslav Pelikan, urged his co-religionists to return to the traditional Christian view of Our Lady, whom Luther called "the foremost" among the saints. Honoring Mary is a "way of emphasizing, not obscuring the centrality of Christ alone," he declared. "She is called the Mother of God not only by the ancient Church but by the Reformation creeds and confessions, because that is a way of asserting that the holy Child of the holy Mother is nothing less than the Second Person of the Blessed Trinity. Where He is thus honored, she must be acknowledged as Mother of God; and where she is rejected, there the centrality of Christ is not enhanced but threatened."

He stated that the attitude of most Protestants today is "far from the spirit and intent" of Luther's Reformation.

He said that he was advocating devotion to Mary in terms compatible with Lutheranism, and not necessarily identical with Catholic teaching and practice.

Dr. Pelikan declared that the faith and trust of the Blessed Virgin "can help us fight the temptation—to rely upon ourselves, our piety, our morality, our right doctrine, rather than solely and utterly upon the action of God." He added that increased respect for Our Lady would "also make its contribution to the healing of the wounds in the body of Christ." We fully agree that Our Lady aids in the restoration of men to unity with Christ, though we consider the Mystical Body in a different sense than most non-Catholics.

Many Lutheran and Anglican churches in Europe and in the United States have statues and paintings of Our Lady. In England, non-Catholics often go on pilgrimage to Marian shrines, pray the rosary, and keep her feast days. In the Soviet Zone in Bernau, near Berlin, an altar of the Blessed Virgin has been restored and reinstalled in the Lutheran Church of St. Mary. It shows Our Lady being crowned in heaven, surrounded by thirty-five apostles and saints. The church and the altar were damaged during the last war, but the restoration was aided by funds from Swedish Lutherans. These are only a few examples; they do not indicate any large-scale trend, at least, not at the present time. But they may be indications of future development and they engender sanguine hope that through prayer and study our separated brethren will find Our Lady—and her Son too, in the Church He founded for all men.

Augustin Cardinal Bea, S.J., head of the Vatican Secretariat for Promoting Christian Unity, expressed optimism in regard to non-Catholic appreciation of Our Blessed Mother. "We may say," he declared, "that Protestantism has made some progress in the esteem and veneration of the Blessed Virgin as an individual person. It has likewise achieved here and there a greater understanding of the peculiar position of the Mother of Christ in the Church."

In an address for World Sodality Day, May 1, 1961, he cited her interest in the Vatican Council in this fashion. "Mary was the first collaborator in the work of redemption when, in the name of the human race, she gave her consent to the Incarnation of the Word of God, the Saviour of mankind. It was she also who, in the name of all humanity, offered Him to the heavenly Father and who, for this twofold reason, became the Mother of all men. Hence today she could not remain indifferent to the great event of the Ecumenical Council. Just as Mary has aided the Church of her Divine Son with such maternal care throughout the two thousand years of her history, so indeed will she aid her now at this important moment when the Church is preparing for a profound renewal. . . ."

Mary is inseparable from the Church as she is inseparable from Christ. Her role in the Church is symbolized by her presence among the apostles at Pentecost, just as she occupied a prominent position in the Incarnation of the Word and His Redemption of the world on the altar of the Cross. As Fr. V. Mura has written: "In the Church, where by the outpouring of the Holy Ghost the Church was definitely founded, Mary begins to exercise visibly, in the midst of the apostles and the disciples gathered together, a role which she will continue to exercise in a more secret and intimate manner: that of uniting hearts in prayer and of giving life to souls through the merits of her all-powerful intercession."

In another way we may consider Our Lady as the special touchstone of orthodoxy. Mary is not a kind of appendage of Catholic belief and practice; she is the reflection of her Son, and in a secondary way the cornerstone upon which the foundation of the Church rests. Thus wrote

Scheeben: "By her position as Mother of Christ and of Christians Mary shares the quality of the spiritual vine of that portion of mankind which is endowed with grace. We may also regard her in Christ and with Christ as the cornerstone on which the latter rests; more closely, as that cornerstone through which the whole structure is connected with the primary conerstone."

The road to religious unity is long and tedious; but the bridge to aid the crossing is Our Lady. In the early ages of the Church and in medieval times she was called a bridge and so she is, enabling men to bypass the difficulties along the way to heaven. Love of Mary is likewise the means of surmounting the obstacles to reunion. A genuine appraisal of her gifts and character helps to remove many psychological and theological difficulties which beset men's minds and ensnare their souls. Love for Mary is not an obstacle to reunion, but a glorious incentive and influence leading to the One Fold of the One Shepherd.

In this matter of the Blessed Virgin's role in Christian Unity, the thoughts of Fr. Jean Danielou, S.J., are fitting and full of confidence: "The Holy Ghost was given in abundance in the Upper Room because Mary was there; every time when Mary is present the Holy Ghost is poured out with abundance and produces the great works of God. For this reason there is much to be hoped for from the emphasis on Mary in our century, that in the same measure as we turn towards such great mysteries as her Mediation and Assumption, God will, in His own mysterious way, prepare a new descent of the Holy Ghost, a new Pentecost. There again the presence of Mary is a pledge and a promise that the Holy Ghost is coming soon, that the infidels will be converted, and—I am most profoundly convinced—that there will be unity among Christians".

And so there will be, through the prayers, influence and love of Our Lady.

Five ❧ Our Lady and the Unity Apostolate

"The salvation of the world depends upon the preaching of devotion to Mary." —St. Alphonsus Liguori.

In considering Our Lady as the principal patroness of Christian Unity, it is fitting to view her in relation to the special apostolate of prayer for the return of all those outside the Fold of St. Peter. Father Paul, the founder of the Chair of Unity Octave, was especially devoted to the Blessed Mary as the great advocate of Unity whom he saluted as Our Lady of the Atonement. When he wrote his famous letter on Nov. 30, 1907, to Rev. Spencer Jones in England about beginning the Unity Octave, he urged the clergyman to join the Rosary League, established at Graymoor, and observed: "The direction of the whole movement is under Our Lady." Through the years the Graymoor founder was unceasing in his promotion of devotion to the Mother of God, as patroness of Christian Unity, and especially as Our Lady of the Atonement.

Our Blessed Lady has a vital role to play in the purpose of Christ's Church. She belongs to the Church and she is the way by which men enter it. She is a member of the Church, but all men become members through her.

The close relationship between Mary and the Church has been discussed by the famous German theologian of the last century, Matthias Scheeben, in this way:

In general, there exists between Mary's Motherhood and that of the Church so close, complete, and mutual a relation, rather so intrinsic a connection and likeness that one can be known in and with each other. The two are connected and resemble each other by the very fact that they depend upon the Holy Spirit for their fecundity and life, and are thereby intended to communicate a holy and spiritual life. In both cases, moreover, the spiritual motherhood over the redeemed includes a motherhood over Christ Himself and indeed owes its perfection to this factor. For, all other maternal factors of the Church center around that by which she brings forth in her womb the Eucharistic Christ as Head, the sacrifice, and the food of the members of the Mystical Body. But the very fact reveals very specially the more sublime and fundamental character of Mary's Motherhood in comparison with that of the Church, and at the same time the organic connection between the two, as a result of which the Church's maternal activity is exerted because of and by virtue of Mary's Motherhood while Mary carries on her Maternal work in and through the Church.

We shall consider Our Lady in regard to the vast intentions as presented by the Chair of Unity Octave, namely, in her function as Mother in praying and interceding for the Unity of all men outside the Church. Perhaps the present day ecumenical movements, the several prominent ones in Europe and a few in our own country, will be a means of leading souls to the Church. Perhaps the social and political upheavals in the world will drive men to their

81

knees so as to cry out in anguish: "Lord, save us, we perish!" But even more, the veneration of the Mother of God which started as a number of tiny trickles is now beginning to assume the force of a strong stream; may it lead to a mighty torrent so as to bring souls forward to the unity of the Church! Christ endowed the Church with unity as a mark of its authenticity, its universality, and its appeal for all men.

It was a stroke of genius or inspiration or perhaps both, when Father Paul began his Octave of prayer for the conversion of the whole non-Catholic world in 1908. Through the blessing of God, he and his infant Society entered the Catholic Church on October 30, 1909, after the Chair of Unity Octave had been only twice observed. When *The Lamp* began in 1903, it was intended to be an organ of defense for the Papacy and for the validity of Anglican Orders. This dual aim continued until the truth won its victory and Father Paul admitted his untenable position of trying to be a Catholic outside the Church. After his conversion, the aim of the publication became Christian Unity and Missions.

"Unity and Missions" was simply another way of stating that the work must be for the growth of the Mystical Body of the Saviour so that more souls would find spiritual life and light, joy and peace. But it was a unity to be accomplished through the intercession of Mary, the Mother of God. Father Paul must have believed deeply these sentiments of Cardinal Wiseman: "Take away Our Blessed Lady's contribution to the Gospel testimony to Christianity, and you find, not simply a broken link, but the very fastening of the whole chain wanting; not merely a gap, or a break made in the structure, but the foundation gone. The belief in the wonders wrought in the Incarnation, of ages, and of the world, rests upon one point of testimony, a unit, a single voice—that of the Blessed Virgin Mary."

Father Paul began his crusade of prayer for unity under the title of the Church Unity Octave. He did not use the title to please non-Catholics or to compromise on Catholic principle but simply to emphasize the essential oneness of the Church, which is her mark and prerogative bestowed by Jesus Christ. There were some non-Catholics who stated that the Church prays for unity which is now non-existent; that the one Church will evolve after the struggles and efforts of men to achieve unity are fulfilled. But such premises cannot be admitted, for the Church is one even as God is one, as Christ her Founder is one. The Church prays "That all may be one" even as the Redeemer did, for all those groups and individuals separated from her by heresy, schism, indifference, apostasy, or any other breach. But in time, when the Octave was being confused with non-Catholic enterprises with another end in view, Father Paul suggested that the name be changed. When a correspondent in the London Catholic paper, *The Universe*, attacked the name, Father Paul rallied to defend its Catholic sense. The charge was this: "With regard to the Church Unity Octave . . . it is, of course, clear to Catholics that we are praying for oneness of faith. Therefore, it is a pity that this title was not substituted for the totally misleading one of Church Unity which originated in a Protestant community (since then converted), and is seized upon by Protestants to confirm their theory that there are several Churches. It is unlikely that the American translation conveys the term used by the Head of Christ's One Church in the Latin brief approving the excellent object of the week of prayer."

Father Paul answered plainly. He stated clearly his own position in a fine apology of his own adherence to Catholic Unity. This was his reply:

As Editor of *The Lamp*, the magazine in which

the Octave originated, will you permit me to state that we used the two words, Church-Unity, to describe the character of the Prayer Octave, and primarily to distinguish it from the so-called Christian Unity widely exploited by the Federation of Protestant and other non-Catholic unitive enterprises.

The purpose of the Church Unity Octave was defined from the very first in the columns of *The Lamp* as a period of eight days of prayer: "For the return of all Christians to the Apostolic See." The words quoted above appear in the first published mention of the Octave.

The reason we chose the Feast of the Chair of St. Peter at Rome upon which to begin the Church Unity Octave, was, of course, to emphasize what had been from the first issue of *The Lamp* its *raison d'etre*. This initial number lies before me as I write and the purpose of its publication is summed up in one paragraph as follows: "No apology is needed for the publication of a monthly organ devoted to the eternal principle of Church Unity laid as the Foundation Stone of the mighty Superstructure, saying: 'Thou art Peter and on this Rock, I will build My Church and the gates of hell shall not prevail against it!'"

As defined by the magazine that originated it, the "Church Unity Octave" means simply an eight-day period of prayer for the return of all separated Christians to the Unity of the Catholic Church. If anyone can provide a substitute title conveying the same thing in as brief a compass, and impossible of misinterpretation, perhaps the Holy Father will accept it in place of the present title, which the Holy Father has approved.

... If our separated brethren, whether of the East or the West, are to be irresistibly drawn by the voice

of the Good Shepherd back to the One Fold from which
their ancestors departed many generations ago, it will
no doubt be because the charity of the Sacred Heart
will find its human medium of expression not alone in
the Vicar of Christ and the Chief Shepherds united
with him, but also in the great body of the Catholic
Faithful.

In 1926, Father Paul learned that Francis Cardinal
Bourne of Westminster favored a change in the name of
Church Unity Octave, for the religious situation was particularly delicate in England shortly after the widely publi-
cized Malines Conference of 1923. The Octave was known
and used by Catholics prior to this time, but with sentiments similar to those expressed by Bishop Dunn, who
wrote: "Some years ago when I first heard of the Unity
Octave, I had it specially observed in my cathedral because
I liked it. But it did not 'catch on' so I dropped it. If it
should be recommended and encouraged by the hierarchy
as a body, I would willingly revive it and propagate it
through my diocese, but in a matter of this sort, it is not
much use trying to act alone."

The Bishops of England approved the Octave in most
of the dioceses, but as a private devotion. Cardinal Bourne,
who personally favored the movement, feared that the words
"Church" and "Unity" would cause great difficulties at that
time because of the action of some of the Anglo-Catholics
in England. The Bishops wished to promote prayer for our
separated brethren, but not at the risk of seeming to compromise on principle.

After the criticism of the name of the Octave, Father
Paul gave "the matter all the more prayerful consideration
in order to offer the Cardinal an alternate title". But it was
Mother Lurana who suggested that name, Chair of Unity
Octave, and Father Paul mentioned the fact in a letter to

the Cardinal (May 29, 1926): "I think the solution of the problem, however, has been granted to the Mother Foundress of the Sisters of the Atonement, Mother Lurana Mary Francis, S.A., after specially invoking the Holy Ghost during the Whitsuntide Octave. She received on yesterday, St. Augustine's Day, the Apostle of England and the first Archbishop of Canterbury, an answer to her prayer which, I trust, Your Eminence will approve of. It seems to me personally like a real inspiration of the Holy Ghost, namely, to substitute for the words 'Church Unity Octave' the name 'Chair of Unity Octave', a title no one could misunderstand."

Very aptly the oration for the feast of St. Augustine expressed this prayer for Unity: "O God, who didst vouchsafe to illumine the English people with the light of the true faith by the preachings and miracles of Blessed Augustine, Thy confessor and Bishop, grant that, by his intercession, the hearts of those who err may return to the unity of the truth that we may be of one mind through Thy Will."

Later, when Cardinal Bourne favored the alternate title, Father Paul commented in *The Lamp*: "This preference of the Cardinal Archbishop of Westminster is most welcome to the originators of the Octave at Graymoor. The Friars of the Atonement believe, in fact, that in a very short time, Chair of Unity Octave will prevail over the more familiar name and supersede it in general acceptance. It is a more explicit description of the kind of Church Unity we desire and pray for. Outside the Church, every man has his own theory and conception of Church Unity; the title 'Chair of Unity' definitely declares that communion with the Chair of Peter at Rome is the only infallible and unfailing test of Catholic Unity."

The old title, Church Unity Octave, persisted however, until 1949, when ecclesiastical authorities in Rome asked that it be changed. The suggestion was made presumably because of unfortunate translations in Latin and Italian. It was officially changed to Chair of Unity Octave at this time by the Society of the Atonement. The present-day title is appropriate, since the Chair of Unity is the Chair of St. Peter at Rome, the symbol of that Unity which Christ gave his Church and which can never fail. As St. Leo the Great says, the faithful should celebrate the Feast of the Chair of St. Peter with as much devotion as they celebrate the day of his martyrdom. "By a moral miracle, which is among the most splendid proofs of the Divine origin of Christianity, Peter still lives and teaches in his successor, and the voice of truth coming from the *Chair of Unity*, reaches to the extremities of the world . . ." (Archbishop Francis Kenrick).

The Octave was first blessed by Pope St. Pius X on December 27, 1909, the feast of the Beloved Apostle who recorded Christ's prayer for Unity, (John c. 17). Father Paul had written to Fr. Herman Walmlesly, S.J., to ask for the Holy Father's blessing on the Octave. Father Walmlesly in turn asked Fr. T. M. Brandi, S.J., editor of *Civilta Cattolica*, to take up the matter in an audience with the Holy Father. Within several days, Father Brandi wrote to Father Walmlesly these encouraging words: "With His whole heart, Pope Pius had blessed the said Father Paul, the 'Institute of the Society of the Atonement' and its work. The Holy Father, moreover, gave a special blessing to the Octave of Prayer for Unity and wished it great success." The note was then forwarded to the Graymoor founder.

Twice each year the Society of the Atonement had sent a Peter's Pence Collection to Rome, on the feast of the Chair of St. Peter, January 18, and the feast of St. Peter in Chains, August 1. Cardinal Merry del Val wrote a note conveying his gratitude to the Graymoor religious. He told them that Pope Pius X was praying for their conversion.

When they sent their small offering in January, 1910, just a few months after their reception into the Church, they received the usual courteous reply. It came on February 24th addressed to Mother Lurana: "In reply to your letter on the 18th inst. I desire to thank you on behalf of the Holy Father for your generous offering of Peter's Pence. His Holiness feels sure that the spirit of attachment to the See of Peter by which the members of the Society of the Atonement were animated and their generosity in this regard have helped in obtaining for them the Divine Mercy, the great grace of conversion to the true faith. The Holy Father, moreover, most cordially bestows His Apostolic Benediction upon you and on each member of your pious community, with the hope that it may be to all a pledge of choicest heavenly favors . . ."

It is remarkable that St. Pius should have blessed the Octave. Only a few generations before, the very prayer used by the Association of Prayer for Unity (A.P.U.C.) in England was proscribed by Pope Pius IX for Catholics because of the ambiguous tenets of the Association; that is, at least by implication that the true faith was no better than any other religion. However, St. Pius was most remarkable, and so was Father Paul.

Pope Benedict XV granted his blessing to the Unity Octave through the Papal Brief, *Romanorum Pontificum*, of February 25, 1916, extended it to the universal Church and augmented it with indulgences. In 1950, the Missionary Union of the Clergy, established in more than fifty countries and numbering more than three hundred and fifty thousand priests, held its third international conference at the Gregorianum University in Rome. One of the chief topics discussed was the problem of the return of all separated brethren to the one true Catholic Church. The following resolution was formulated: "Let the efforts be multiplied that our separated brothers return to the one true Church of Christ, and that the sheep that are lost of the house of Israel be led back to the faith. Let the Octave for Unity— from the 18th to the 25th of January—be celebrated in all parishes; moreover, let a week or at least a day for the Christian Orient be celebrated in the seminaries."

Through the blessings of God and the favor of the Church the Octave has spread rapidly and widely. It is observed among millions of the faithful all over the world, in Africa, India and China, in the small mission chapels and in the great cathedrals and churches of Europe and America. It is the gigantic response to the plea of Father Paul to observe the Chair of Unity Octave and to beseech the Father of mercies through the intercession of Our Lady to lead home "the erring brethren".

It has impressed us that love of the Church and the Pope and devotion to Mary are joined together inseparably. Those who love the Vicar of Christ are most devoted to Mary; while those who are careless toward their profession of this belief are negligent in their filial duties to their Spiritual Mother. Cardinal Suenens has written well on this point: "To love Mary is to love the Pope and receive his commands with respect, gratitude, and joy. 'Lord, to whom shall we go?' asked the apostles, 'Thou hast the words of eternal life'. Peter, living amongst us, is still the final refuge, the light which deceives not. Love of Mary is love of the bishop who, in his local Church, is the representative of Christ amongst us. 'He that heareth you heareth Me', said Jesus. With that in mind, we shall not stress his weakness or his deficiencies, but shall see in him the shepherd of the sheep, the genuine teacher of religious truth. Love of Mary is love of the priest whom we encounter daily . . ."

As the noted convert, Father Louis Bouyer, C. Orat., has observed: "Mary, at the beginning of the Church, represents as concentrated in one person the same perfection that will be displayed finally in the multitude of believers gathered together in Unity. She is the symbol and the pledge of Catholic Unity."

It is not by chance or coincidence that Our Lady is mentioned in three stages of the Church's formation; at the Incarnation, the Redemption, and Pentecost. Thus, the mystery of the Church is also the mystery of Mary. As Father Terrien has said: "Although both conceived by the Holy Ghost and although this spirit of God made both fruitful, Mary to be the Mother of Christ and His Members, the Church to bring forth children of adoption, for fear of offending either, we should not venture to attribute to the Church the inexpressible fulness of the Holy Ghost which we acknowledge in Our Lady: for the Church herself receives from Mary's fulness as Mary shares in Christ's ... That is the meaning of the phrase used by the Fathers: "The Church imitates the Mother of Christ—*Ecclesia imitatur Matrem Christi* ... Thus, the Son of God created the Church in the likeness of His own Mother. God is not an image of man, but man is of God: likewise the Church is the image of Mary, not Mary of the Church."

In the following pages we will give a brief explanation of the various and vast intentions of the Unity Apostolate as listed by the Unity Octave. These eight great enterprises make up the gigantic missionary apostolate of the Church —to bring into the Unity of faith, worship and government all who are separated from her in every part of the world. For in the words of Pope John XXIII: "Then the horizon broadens: 'And other sheep I have that are not of this fold ...' Here is the missionary problem in all its vastness and beauty. This is the solicitude of the Roman Pontiff, the primary one ..."

1. *The union of all Christians in the one true faith and in the Church.*

The extension of the kingdom of God upon earth depends upon every Catholic, not just upon the priest, the religious or the bishop. Everyone, whether a renowned prelate or a humble factory worker, housewife or business executive, student or professor—has the duty of making Christ known and loved through the world.

To bring Christ and His love into the lives of other men is the duty of every soul sealed with the Sacrament of baptism and anointed with the oil of confirmation. "It is no use pleading the duties and requirements of our state of life which monopolize the existence and activities of man in this world," writes Cardinal Suenens, "as if the first duty of the Christian were not that which derives from Baptism and makes him responsible for his neighbor! And his neighbor means not merely his own family. Our age is marked by fear of responsibility. This is tantamount to saying it is profoundly 'dechristianized'. The baptized layman ought to understand that the apostolate is a normal, elementary duty, something which stands to reason and that the only permissible question is the precise form it will take. It is sometimes thought that the life of Our Lord is a model for the clergy alone, and not for every Christian; that is a fatal, pernicious error. Since Christ was to the highest degree an apostle, it follows that every Christian, a member of Christ, should also be one. The popes in reminding the laity of the urgent need for Catholic action have introduced no real novelty into the Church, nor propounded some 'new organization'. It is not an addition suddenly imposed on the twentieth century action; it has been from the very beginning an imperative duty, the need for which compels more than ever urgent recognition."

At times some people say that it is not the Church's mission to convert the world, but to make the Christian life desirable and possible for all men. They say the word 'convert' does not appear at all in Christ's missionary instructions. In answer we must say that the whole tenor of the New Testament teaching is about a change of life—from sin to grace, from error to truth, from hatred to love. And just as Our Divine Lord was radical in the sense of turning upside-down and inside-out the ideas and attitudes of men, teaching them that nothing matters except the salvation of their souls, so the Church in the world today constantly preaches His doctrine of repentance, of atonement, and a readjustment of values in terms of God and eternal life. The Church does want to convert the world; it is her function, her mission, the very purpose of her existence.

And the Church will fulfill its mission—by the will of God and through the intercession and love of the Blessed Virgin Mary.

Those who are apostles, who strive to bring the good news of salvation to those outside the Church, or to win back those who were once members, must be devoted to Our Lady in order to bring souls to the Saviour. As Father Olier used to say: "Mary does not perform outwardly the function of an apostle, although she received it in its fulness. She is not concerned with Jew or gentile in particular but having with her the fulness of her Son's zeal and power over the Church, she possesses also, through her eminent participation in Jesus Christ, both the zeal for God's glory and the power to send secretly, by the channels of the Holy Ghost and divine love, God's servants throughout the world."

If all Catholics were convinced of their role in the salvation of other men, what a tremendous spiritual change would bless the world. Bishop Francis Xavier Ford of Maryknoll, who died in China for the faith in 1952, wrote of the Unity Octave: "If Catholics . . . were to redouble their prayers for the conversion of those outside the fold, the united prayers that would storm heaven would without doubt mark the year of the Pentecostal renewal. Our participation in this Octave would at least enlarge our viewpoint, broaden our charity, and make us see in every man a brother whom Christ is yearning to welcome to His Sacraments." To this he added: "Our Blessed Mother wants us to share anxiety for the conversion of the world ... she wants us to carry about with us in our daily work this deep anxiety for the conversion of souls, and a corresponding generosity in offering reparation for the sins of the world ... Our hearts must be like the Heart of Mary; anxiously yearning for the conversion of all people."

Our Divine Lord gave the positive order to convert the world: Teach all nations. The excuse of non-intervention can claim no authority from the Saviour. And the thought of St. Paul should echo deep in men's souls: "Woe to me if I do not preach the Gospel" (1 Cor. 9:16). St. Chrysostom had a word for those who feared to answer the call of the apostolate: "Among other duties you have that of devoting yourselves to the salvation of your brethren, of leading them to us despite their resistance, cries, and complaints. The opposition and indifference are proof that you are dealing with children. It is for you to change the imperfect and sorry dispositions of their souls. It is your duty to coax them to become men." Every Catholic has the obligation of working for the extension of the kingdom of Christ, of sacrificing to save souls. Numbers matter little, and the method of cooperation with the Redemption varies according to the differences of vocation, but each individual has his own particular part to fill, and if the whole world is to be saved, each Christian must be faithful to the care of the souls entrusted to him by God.

Our Lady has constantly made known her desire for the conversion of sinners. At La Salette, at Fatima, Beauraing, and Lourdes, the Mother of God has put forth the same message: Prayer and penance for the conversion of sinners. Mary is, as it were, the voice of God speaking to the world, to men who will listen to the indispensable means of bringing men to God. Mary calls her faithful children to pray and to do penance for the conversion of the unfaithful, for the return of those who have fallen away, and for the religious unity of all men with God.

Though the problem of reunion is staggering and the task seems almost impossible, the gentle but powerful influence of Mary will overcome the forces of evil and disunity. Mary is not only the humble Maid of Nazareth, but the great sign in heaven, the woman clothed with the sun, formidable as an army ready for battle—and she will overcome the powers of hell and win souls to God. As Pope Pius XI declared: "May Mary, the most holy Queen of the Apostles, graciously second our common undertakings; Mary, since she holds in her Mother's heart all men who were committed to her on Calvary, cherishes and loves not only those who happily enjoy the fruits of the Redemption, but those likewise who still do not know that they have been redeemed by Jesus Christ."

Mary's role of uniting men with God is inseparably bound up with the purpose of the Church. She is the Mother of the Head of the Mystical Body and of all His members as well. As Pope Pius XII has stated: "It was she who was immune from all sin, personal or inherited, and ever most closely united with her Son, offered Him on Golgotha to the Eternal Father together with the holocaust of her maternal right and love . . ." The function of the Church and the role of Our Lady is to bring forth members unto Christ the Head, to make them holy, and to lead them to eternal life.

The Most Rev. Francis Charriere, Bishop of Lausanne, Geneva and Fribourg, urged the faithful to greater devotion towards the Mother of God for the sake of Christian Unity in his pastoral letter for Lent during the Marian Year of 1954. He referred to the objections raised in Protestant circles about the Catholic emphasis on Mariology, the criticism of the Marian Year and the claim that devotion to Mary would constitute a barrier to the cause of reunion. But he replied that devotion to Mary is an incentive rather than an impediment to unity: "When the children of a family are separated, it is the role of the Mother to bring them together and reconcile them. Today, as at Cana, Mary can obtain from her Son the miracle which ordinary human efforts are incapable of realizing. But that goal, the unity of the visible Church, demands that we take seriously her directives to the servants at the marriage feast—to do what the Son commands."

So it is the work of our Blessed Lady to "bring together" all her children and to "reconcile" those who are separated from the Church. She continues the work of ministering to souls through every century, and the more she is exalted, the more does the Church flourish. It is the duty of her faithful children to imitate her motherly solicitude and to be instruments of grace by love and prayer in winning to the Church those souls now separated from her and from the Unity of the One Fold of her beloved Son.

Our Holy Father, Pope John, reminds us of Our Lady's motherhood of all men. "Mary is the Mother of Christ, the head of all mankind, brothers all in the same first-born Christ. By her maternal solicitude and compassion she contributed to have divine and supernatural life restored to us; and in the person of the beloved disciple she was given to us as our spiritual Mother by Christ Himself on the cross."

2. *The return of separated Eastern Christians to communion with the Holy See.*

The second great intention of the Unity Apostolate compels us to turn to those who have many riches of the

Church, but who fail to possess and enjoy the unity of government which the Divine Master gave to the faithful. These peoples of the Near East, and now spread all over the world, are the racial and cultural descendants of those giants of the early ages of the faith: St. Ignatius of Antioch, St. Justin, St. Irenaeus of Lyons, St. John Chrysostom, St. Basil, St. Athanasius, and a host of other Saints of the East who gloried in the oneness of the Church.

Our Eastern separated brethren have valid sacraments; the holy priesthood by which Calvary is renewed upon the altar for the purpose of uniting men with God; they have a great love for the faith—and they have died for it in countless instances—but at present, they do not possess that loyalty to the Pope, that oneness with the See of St. Peter, which is the mark of the true Catholic. Their difficulties are often more psychological than theological, but whatever the reasons for the barrier, they are still formidable.

They also possess a deep veneration for the holy Mother of God and in this love, it seems, lies the hope of their ultimate union with Christ's Vicar on earth. We note with joy and consolation the love of Eastern peoples for the Virgin Mother. It also seems that when Russia is converted —and it will be—the task will be achieved less by the priests of the Latin rite than those of the Byzantine rite, whose ancestry and culture resemble closely the suffering millions behind the Iron Curtain.

In the Byzantine liturgy (used by the Ukranians, Ruthenians, Melkites or Syrians, Rumanians, Italo-Greeks, Russians and numerous Orthodox of various national origins), the litanies and invocations conclude with this commemoration of love for their Queen: "Remembering our all-holy, immaculate, most blessed and glorious lady, the Mother of God and the Ever-Virgin Mary, and all the saints, we commend ourselves and one another and all our life to God." At the commemoration of the saints the following

Megalynarion (Magnificat Hymn) is sung: "It is truly meek to bless thee, Thou Birthgiver of God, ever blessed and immaculate Mother of God. Honored above the Cherubim, incomparably more glorious than the Seraphim, inviolate Bearer of God the Word, true Mother of God, we magnify thee."

At the end of the Syrian liturgy this blessing is given by the celebrant over the people: "May God . . . be favorably mindful of your dead, and may He watch over you the living, by the prayers and intercession of that Mother clothed in holiness, that second heaven, the sinless Virgin Mother of God, Mary, and of all saints. Amen."

The familiar *Ave Maria* of the Latin rite is not used in public or private prayer among many peoples of the Eastern rites separated from the Church; but some use the Ave in this form: "Hail, Mother of God and Virgin Mary, full of grace, the Lord is with thee. Blessed art thou amongst women and blessed is the fruit of thy womb, for thou hast born Christ, the Saviour of souls." In the Coptic rite of Ethiopia, this form of the Ave occurs in the ordinary text of the liturgy, said alternately by priest and people: "Hail Mary, full of grace, the Lord is with thee. Blessed are thou amongst women, and blessed is the fruit of thy womb. Pray and intercede with thy beloved Son, that He may forgive us our sins."

Almost thirteen hundred years ago in Egypt the same version of the Eastern rite was used. Some Catholics of the Oriental rites use the rosary and give the Ave a different rendering, appropriate to each decade. Thus, "Hail Mary . . . thy womb, Jesus, who suffered for us upon the cross. Amen." The Copts in Egypt sing an office of Our Lady each day of the month of December and have the following prayer in their office of Compline: "Mother of God, if we trust in thee we shall not be shamed but saved. Strengthened by thy help and intercession, Most holy, pure and

97

perfect one, we shall resist temptations and put them to flight. We seek the shelter of thy aid like a strong shield, and we beseech thee, Mother of God, to protect us by thy prayers. Lead us out of the darkness of sin to glorify the Almighty God who took flesh from thee. Amen."

Among the Eastern separated brethren (as well as among Catholics), there is a beautiful and widely known chant in honor of Our Lady. The Akathistos Hymn, a kind of litany interspersed with chants, some of which are sung in the church on the first four Saturdays of Lent and the whole on *Akathistos Saturday,* the fifth Saturday of Lent. It is used for private devotions during the entire year. It has been translated into all the liturgical languages, i.e., Church Slavonic, Rumanian, Arabic, and into Latin, Italian, German, Russian, French, Ukrainian, and other tongues.

This work (or something similar to it) is believed to have been composed on the occasion of the deliverance of Constantinople from the barbarians in 626 A.D. There are many express references to Our Lady and her role in uniting men with Christ and in preserving their unity in the Church. "Hail, Bride Unwedded", is the recurrent phrase throughout. "To thee, unconquered Queen, I, thy city from danger freed, an offering of thanks inscribe. O Birth-giver of God! Yet for thy unconquerable might free me from all hurt that I may sing to thee:

Hail! Bride unwedded . . .
Hail! sinful Adam's recalling.
Hail! Eve's tears redeeming.
Hail! earthly bridge carrying the earthborn unto heaven.
Hail! Mother of Lamb and Shepherd.
Hail! fold of rational sheep.
Hail! against unseen foes defending.

Hail! the heavenly gateway's opening.
Hail! of faith the firm foundation.
Hail! of Grace the shining token ...
Hail! thou hast quenched the fire of error.
Hail! thou who enlightenest the initiates of the Triune.
Hail! thou who hast redeemed us from pagan rites.
Hail! thou who rescuest us from works of mire.
Hail! thou who has quenched the cult of fire.
Hail! thou who raisest mankind up.
Hail! thou who castest demons down.
Hail! thou who the fraud of idols has trodden 'neath
thy feet.

Father Vincent McNabb, O.P., has commented on
this beautiful piece of Marian literature: "Without a doubt
the East had more reason than had the West for keeping
Mary the Mother of God in the forefront, we might also
say the battlefront, of its praise. The enemy who almost
compassed the death of Jesus of Nazareth pursued the infant Church with unabated zeal and intelligence. In the
Greek-speaking East he launched an attack in force first
against the divinity of the Son made flesh. There were
moments in that great attack when the enemy of Christ
seemed to conquer. But finally at Ephesus his hundred
years' war against the Son of Mary was broken by the
Greek-speaking East's proclaiming the Mother of that Son
to be *Theotokos*, Forthbringer or Mother of God.
"Such memories of victories won clung to the Mother,
in whose arms her Son was safe, that their gentle highland
Maid was looked upon as a thing invulnerable—a tower
of hardest ivory, the Tower of David. Thus, it became a
fashion of Christian faith and love to meet all attacks
against the faith as Ephesus met them by invoking the
Theotokos. Such invocation was the highest act of faith,

99

not in the divinity of the human mother, but in the divinity of her human Son. Ten centuries of stress had not withered that faith when the Christian East in a day of deliverance from invasion chanted in Sancta Sophia the splendid praise which now is given her in the speech of Our Lady's Dowry."

Even though the Orthodox people have a deep love for Mary, some have repudiated the Marian dogmas defined by the Pope, the Immaculate Conception in 1854 and the Assumption in 1950. As noted before, their rejection is founded not on any disloyalty to Mary but on a reaction against the "Bishop of Rome". Still, we have the utmost confidence that Our Lady will bring back these, her people, to the unity of the Church and they will confess their allegiance to the Supreme Pontiff as the Vicar of the Son of God upon earth. The images of Our Lady in the East, Our Lady of Blakhernae, and Our Lady who Guides (Bodigitria), and Our Lady of Vladimir so beloved in Russia, will help fan the flames of devotion in the hearts of the Eastern people separated from the Holy See. It is significant too that the popular images in the Western Church, Our Lady of Good Counsel, Our Lady of Perpetual Help, and Our Lady of Czestochowa, are of Eastern origin. In the providence of God may the prophecy of the saintly Conventual Friar, Fr. Maximilian Kolbe, be fulfilled: "One day you will see the statue of the Immaculate atop the Kremlin."

For the present, Mary's love has to remain hidden and confined in Russia and other Communist-dominated lands. But the day is coming ever closer when the devotion of the people for their *Bogoroditza* (She-Who-Gave-Birth-to-God) will rise again, and they can pour out their love for the Queen and Mother in demonstrations of joy and protestations of gratitude. Mary will win the world for Christ— she will bring men to the unity of the One Fold of her beloved Son and Savior.

3. *The reconciliation of Anglicans with the Holy See.*

When we pray for the return of the Anglicans and Episcopalians (and Protestant Episcopalians) and of the various 'Church' groups to which they belong, whether "high, low, broad", it is with a sense of wistfulness. Prior to its separation from Rome in the sixteenth century, England was so devoted to the Mother of God as to merit the title: "Dowry of Mary" (*Dos Mariae*). But all that is changed now. In those places of veneration which filled the valleys and crowned the hillsides of England, in Canterbury, Ely, Lincoln, Worchester, York, there is no sound of the *Salve Regina* or the *Regina Coeli.* Even the famed Walsingham is relatively silent; its Catholic chant is but a small echo of what the glorious veneration of Mary once was. No king ever began his reign with a greater devotion to this shrine than Henry VIII; but later he plundered the holy spot and stripped its sanctuary of gems and precious metals. The single wall standing starkly alone is mute reminder of what one man did because he flung aside the love of the Mother of God in lust for creatures and in greed for power.

With the sad king's perfidy came a whole legion of evils. Persecution and apostasy, confiscation of lands by those who had no right to them, mob violence and vandalism, and worst of all, the loss of millions to the faith that once was so dear, and the rejection of the Mother of God who had been so lovingly honored. It was a tragic page in the history of England and of the world when a monarch turned from God and His Holy Mother to plunge a whole nation and succeeding generations away from the true Church, and away from the embrace of a Mother's love. But the end is not yet, and Mary's star is beginning to rise once more.

More than one hundred years ago the great Newman

portrayed the sorry fate of apostasy from God and separation from the Church. In tones that made the prelates and clergy of England weep, the famous convert recalled the story of England's spiritual defection. (Sermon of "Second Spring")

Three centuries ago, the Catholic Church, that great creation of God's power, stood in this land in pride of place. It had the honors of near a thousand years upon it; it was enthroned in some twenty Sees up and down the broad country; it was based in the will of a faithful people; it energized through ten thousand instruments of power and influence; and it was ennobled by a host of saints and martyrs ... Mixed with the civil institutions, with kings and nobles, with the people found in every village and town—it seemed destined to stand, so long as England stood, and to outlast, it might be, England's greatness.

But the change came; the holy faith became contemptible and the love of Mary despicable. The great abbeys and cathedrals became the pawns of those who could seize and destroy; the souls of men were bereft of that knowledge and love of the Most High God, while the few Catholics who remained became a kind of foolish curiosity in the land, as Newman described them:

Such was about the sort of knowledge possessed of Christianity by the heathen of old times, who persecuted its adherents from the face of the earth, and then called them a *gens lucifuga*, a people who shunned the light of day. Such were the Catholics in England, found in corners and alleys and cellars, and the housetops, or in the recesses of the country, cut off from the populous world around them, and dimly seen, as

102

through mist of twilight, as ghosts flitting to and fro, by the high Protestants, the lords of the earth. At length, so feeble did they become, so utterly contemptible, that contempt gave birth to pity; and the more generous of their tyrants actually began to wish to bestow on them favor, under the notion that their opinions were simply too absurd to spread again, and that they themselves, were they but raised in civil importance, would unlearn and be ashamed of them.

Then Newman turned from the past and present to the future. He prayed for the coming of Mary upon the blighted land. She would usher in the coming of the "Second Spring," her era of triumph and glory. "It is the time for thy Visitation. Arise, Mary, and go forth in thy strength into that north country, which once was thine own and take possession of a land which knows thee not." And he continued:

> Arise, Mother of God, and with thy thrilling voice, speak to those who labor with child and are in pain, till the babe of grace leaps within them! Shine on us, dear Lady, with thy bright countenance, like the sun in his strength, *O stella matutina,* O harbinger of peace, till our year is one perpetual May. From thy sweet eyes, from thy pure smile, from thy majestic brow, let ten thousand influences rain down, not to confound or overwhelm, but to persuade, to win over thine enemies. O Mary, my hope, O Mother undefiled, fulfill to us the promise of this spring.

Newman declared that in the new age, saints and doctors and preachers and martyrs would reconsecrate the land to God. And so it shall be. The number of Catholic converts among the Anglicans is not vast, but it is significant. Much of Protestant England is becoming either non-religious or Catholic. Some bishops of the Anglican body scorn Catholic devotion to the Mother of God; they reject love for her as a model of holy purity. They do not know that Mary is God's instrument in the world to bring all mankind to Him. It may well be that the affliction that some English rulers forced upon Ireland was the way of Divine Providence to bring the proud nation back to the faith, for even now a large part of the Catholic clergy come from Ireland and many of the faithful migrated from their homeland to Britain in search of a livelihood, bringing with them the true faith.

Each year witnesses an increasing number of converts. But that number, about fifteen thousand annually, is a small proportion of the population of more than forty million non-Catholics. But we do not try to balance numbers with numbers. Statistics may be of some assistance in estimating the task to be done, but the answer to conversion is prayer, prayer, and prayer. For only from prayer will come forth the apostolic zeal to sacrifice and to seek for souls outside the Fold of the Divine Redeemer.

In 1950 the Carmelite friars took over a monastery at Aylesford which had been their possession until the Protestant revolt. Our Lady appeared to St. Simon Stock at this place in 1251; she was accompanied by angels and promised that those who would wear the Brown Scapular would not suffer eternal loss. It is significant that these friars should return to their monastery during that "Year of the Great Return", the Holy Year, and at the time that the Assumption was declared a dogma of the Holy Church revealed by God.

We pray that Our Lady will regain other portions of her Dowry. Two ideas are connoted by the word "dowry" when we speak of the *Dos Mariae*, but only one applies to Our Lady. When we refer to England as "The Dowry of Mary" we do not mean the gift which a bride brings her husband at marriage, or anything analogous to it. We mean that England was assigned to Mary as a permanent gift which no one could take away. Hence, England rightfully belongs to Mary, and though violent hands of the Protestant Revolt robbed her of it, it is still lawfully her own. The first actual offering of England to Mary seems to have been made by Edward III. When Cardinal Wiseman in 1867, and Cardinal Vaughn in 1893, reconsecrated England to Mary, they were repeating in substance an act that had been made from the time of King Edward. His grandson, Richard II, confirmed the gift. In the English College at Rome there is an ancient painting showing Richard and his queen on their knees, offering through the hands of St. John their country to the Blessed Virgin. Below are inscribed the words: *"Dos tua, Virgo pia, haec est; quare rege Maria*—This, O Holy Virgin is thy dowry; do thou, O Mary, reign over us."

In the words of Pope Leo XIII we pray for the English nation and for all those who belong to the Episcopal communion, in America, Canada, India, in the Philippines and Japan, and in all parts of the world.

O Blessed Mother of God and our own most gentle Queen and Mother, look down in mercy upon England thy dowry and upon all who gently hope and trust in thee. By thee Jesus our Saviour and our help was given to the world; and He has given thee to us that we might hope still more. Plead for us, thy children, whom thou didst receive and accept at the foot of the cross. O Sorrowful Mother! intercede for our separated brethren that they may be united with us in the one fold of the supreme shepherd, the Vicar of thy Son. Pray for us, dear Mother, that by faith fruitful in good works we may all deserve to see and praise God together with thee in our heavenly home.

Before becoming a Catholic Father Paul spoke to Cardinal Gibbons of Baltimore in 1909. He mentioned the conversion of the Anglicans, and the prelate answered: "If we had the Anglicans with us we could convert the world." Surely Catholics should be vitally interested in this group of people, now cut off from the Church to which their ancestors belonged, who were so prominent in love for the Mother of God.

In April, 1947, a beautiful figure of Our Lady of Walsingham was presented to Pope Pius XII by a party of British Forces. In reply to the presentation the Holy Father said:

> It was certainly a very happy and pious thought that prepared the presentation to us of a statue of Our Lady of Walsingham. We really find it difficult to express how pleased we are with this gift. It brings to us England's Loretto. It quickens remembrance of the joy that filled the soul of Mary when Gabriel said at Nazareth—Ave!
>
> We shall keep it close to Our Person and when Our eyes rest on it, there will rise from Our heart a fervent prayer that the Blessed Mother may win the favor of her divine Son for you who have had the pleasure of making this presentation and the privilege of affording Us a deep and holy joy; a prayer for those, too, whom We represent in a special way, and for all the Catholics of the realm: yes, and for all the English nation and its gracious Sovereign.

Because Our Lady of Walsingham belongs to England, and it was the 15th century poet laureate of the celebrated chapel now long since destroyed, who sang, that England belongs to Mary:

O England, great cause thou hast to be
Compared to the land of promise, Sion:
Thou attainest by grace to stand in that degree
Through this glorious Lady's supportation.
To be called in every realm and region
The holy land, Our Lady's Dowry.
Thus art thou named of old antiquity.

Dare one doubt that Our Lady still looks down with motherly love on the island where for centuries innumerable pilgrims came to lay aside their burdens at her shrine: "where grace is daily showed to men of every age" and departing carried within the inner reaches of their souls a heavenly peace, born of a child-like faith, which heals the heart and draws the veil from before the vision of pure, unending joy?

The love of a mother is ever fruitful; her prayers are truly efficacious. Mary will win back her Dowry to the faith as well as other peoples in the Anglican communion. Mary's reign is over the souls of men. She will persuade; she will influence; she will reign. May her hour come quickly!

4. *The reconciliation of European Protestants with the Holy See.*

This intention furnishes the fourth great object of prayer for Unity. The Lutherans today consitute a body of nearly seventy million members in various parts of the world, fifty million of them in continental and northern Europe. The Calvinists in France and Switzerland, in Holland and Belgium, comprise a number of about ten million. The present interest in Our Lady shown by a number of Protestants, particularly among those of the Lutheran confession, is an indication that they are coming closer to Catholic truth, and once they learn to love and respect Mary, they will begin their return to the Church.

Even as a young priest, Martin Luther could write these poetic words about the Mother of God: "If I had as many tongues as there are stars in the sky, or grains of sand on the seashore, or leaves of all the forests, and with all these tongues I did nothing but praise Mary day and night, I could never say anything half so glorious to her as that which is expressed in the single phrase: 'Thou art the Mother of God.'"

But before long the unfortunate friar repudiated devotion to his Mother and broke from the Church. Among his followers, however, veneration of Our Lady did not die quickly. In many places in the sixteenth century Lutherans continued to observe the feast of the Assumption of Mary with festivals and gatherings, because the people loved the feast. And at the present day, many show their love for Our Lady by reciting her rosary; there has been a notable increase in Marian devotion, especially in the Evangelical Church of Mainz. An indication of a trend, perhaps, even in America, is the fact that a Lutheran church in Reading, Pennsylvania, now has an outdoor statue of Our Lady as the Mother of God.

During the Holy Year of 1950 a Lutheran minister, Richard Baumann, made a pilgrimage to Rome. In writing of his experiences, he frequently referred to the Blessed Virgin. Of her rosary, he stated: ... "when the rosary is said, truth sinks into the subconscious like a slow and steady downpour, the hammering sentences of the catechism receive an indelible validity precisely for the little ones." He made special note of the fact that the symbolical books of the Evangelical Lutheran Church use many expressions of praise for Our Lady: "Mary the pure, the holy, the ever-virgin, the God-bearer, truly the Mother of God, worthy of amplest praise. She wills that we follow her example. She prays for the Church."

Max Thurian, widely known theologian of the Reformed Church of France, recently made a statement, which if accepted generally would revolutionize the theology of his religious body. Writing of the communion of saints, he concluded with this reference to Our Lady:

> In the Communion of the Holy Supper, we must be equally conscious that it unites us not only to our brothers communicating with us, but to the whole Church; such is the meaning of the commemoration of the saints in the Canon of the Mass, Finally, intercession strengthens the sense of *koinonia* (fellowship). It would not make sense for reformed doctrine to pray for those who have died within the communion of the Church. We do not pray for saints who now rest in Christ; why do we not ask that of those who live close to Him? They are no more separated from us than when they were alive. St. Paul or St. Peter or Mary are as near to us as they were to their contemporaries in the Church. To ask their intercession with God no more devaluates the unique intercession of Christ, than to ask here on earth the prayers of a brother for oneself, or to intercede for others. The great litany of the saints is the most moving and strongest ecumenical prayer. And Mary is present at the head of this general assembly and the Church of the firstborn whose names are written in heaven.

Recently, four German Lutheran theologians wrote a treatise on the Church, revealing an awareness of their condition outside the Catholic Church. It read: "In that we dispense ourselves in large measure from the deposit of truth held by the apostles and the prophets, do we have the right to conceal the truth that grace works in the created order and that consequently it comes to us through created realities? Who gives us, after all, the authority to suppress insistently the doctrine of a reward for good works? And how can we account for the fact that we no longer affirm that the preaching of the Gospel, the priestly function of divine worship, and the martyrdom of Christians are . . . a consequence of the sacrifice of Christ? Why do we allow ourselves to leave the problem of the function of Peter to philosophers and classical scholars? Our want of faith consists precisely in our no longer looking upon the Church except as a reality of this world. Because of this we do not recognize her profound character, and for that very reason we no longer live in communion with the saints and the perfectly righteous."

In Germany a common front against the Nazis drove the Catholics and the Protestants together, and they formed a political party. But greater still is the approach of Protestants to the riches of the true faith. Pastor Hans Asmussen has written a book on Our Lady that is close to the Catholic teaching, and other clergymen encourage respect and love for the Mother of God.

In the Lutheran Church of Sweden a ritualistic movement has developed and the ritual has been taken up again in the sense of sacrifice. The ministers wear vestments similar to those of Catholic priests; they direct the worship of God from the altar rather than from the pulpit. Four hundred years have passed since the sons of St. Francis were in Norway; but they too have returned as well as Dominican friars. The lands that gave to the Church its St. Olaf and St. Magnus, St. Hallvard and St. Eyestein, its St. Canute in Denmark, its St. Bridget and St. Catherine of Sweden will again give birth to new saints of the Church. In the Abbey Church of Vadstena in Sweden erected according to directions from St. Brigitta (often known as Bridget) there is the famous statue of the "Beautiful Madonna". It stands both as a memorial of the past and the herald of a new day when the ceremonies and chants of the Catholic Church will again resound throughout the edifice in the future. In Norway, the most beautiful church is that of St. Mary's in Bergen; in the great cathedral of Trondheim the statue of the Virgin and Child stands out prominently. These are remnants of a faith that was lost; may they also stand as a prophecy for the future. Love of Mary will rise again and fan the flame of love for the truth and bring her children to the true fold.

With the prayer of the famous Barnabite priest, Fr. Karl Schilling, who labored so extensively for the conversion of the Lutherans in Scandinavia, we ask a divine blessing upon these peoples to return to the faith of their forefathers.

Remember, O Saviour of the world, that for these souls Thou didst shed Thy Precious Blood and endure untold sufferings. Good Shepherd, lead these Thy flock back to the wholesome pastures of the Church, so that they may be one flock together with us under Thy Vicar here on earth—the Bishop of Rome, who in the person of the Holy Apostle Peter was commissioned by Thee to care both for the lambs and for the sheep.

Hear, O merciful Jesus, these our petitions, which we make to Thee with full trust in the love of Thy Sacred Heart towards us, and to Thy Holy Name be glory, honor, and praise throughout all eternity.

We pray that all the Lutheran peoples of Europe, the Calvinists in France and Switzerland, and other sincere Protestants may come to know the fullness of truth in the

111

One Fold and One Shepherd. When they return home to the true Church it will be through the influence and love of the Queen of the Universe, the all-holy Mother of God.

5. *That American Christians become one in union with the Chair of Peter.*

The object to this intention is particularly close to the faithful of the United States, for our land was dedicated to the Mother of God under the title of the Immaculate Conception in 1847. Its very beginnings were connected with Our Lady. Columbus came here in 1492 in the ship, *Santa Maria,* and named an island to honor the Immaculate Conception. De Soto named the Mississippi River in honor of the Immaculate Conception. Los Angeles was originally the City of Our Lady of the Angels (a famous Franciscan title from the Portiuncula in Assisi), the Chesapeake Bay was called the Bay of the Mother of God, while in Maryland there are St. Mary's County and St. Mary's City.

In later times we find the names of towns such as Maryville, Marysville, Maryvale, Conception, Mount Carmel, Santa Maria, and similar ones testifying to the glory of Our Lady and the devotion of the faithful towards her. We believe that the Church in our country will burst forth into its "First Spring." Its potential for greatness is tremendous, not simply in terms of military might and space age progress, but spiritually it is capable of the greatest achievement in love for God and in devotion to His Mother.

At present, more than twenty-one thousand churches in the United States are named in honor of Mary, with a wide variety of titles: Our Lady of Lake Huron, on the shores of the Great Lakes; Our Lady of the Ozarks in the southern part of our country; Our Lady of the Mountains, in Nevada; Our Lady of the Springs, in Colorado, and Our Lady of the Redwoods in California. Other sections of the country bear witness to devotion to the Virgin Mother as Our Lady of the Hills, Our Lady of the Isle, and Our Lady of Good Harbor in New England. All over America there are many indications of love for Mary, some of them remnants from the past, while others, we trust, foreshadow the future filled with greater devotion to the holy Virgin.

There are one hundred and ninety million people in the United States, but only forty-five million are members of the Catholic Church. Some of those outside the Church are members of Eastern Orthodox groups, and of the Jewish faith, but the vast majority of our countrymen are Protestants or so they profess to be; even if they do not regularly attend religious services, they consider themselves and are considered Protestants.

A few facts about the Protestants in America may be helpful. They number sixty-four million, or about one-third of the population. The principal groups are the Methodists, Lutherans, Baptists, and Episcopalians, and these are subdivided into many groups. For example, there are twenty-five Baptist bodies, twenty-one Methodist groups, eleven Presbyterian, and eighteen Lutheran. There are two hundred and fifty Protestant sects in America and each has almost countless subdivisions.

But while we pray for all these Protestant groups separated from the Church, we also pray for other bodies not ordinarily considered part of the Protestant persuasion, such as the Jehovah's Witnesses, whose zeal is well known, the Mormons, who now number more than a million members, with a significant increase within the past ten years, the Christian Scientists, and so on. Our Lady is the Mother of all these people, longing to bring them to the unity of the Church of her Divine Son.

If the Catholic laity of our nation were fired with the dignity and glory of their vocation as lay apostles, the Church would make tremendous strides in a very short time.

Indeed, if each Catholic brought just one person into the Church each year, in a period of three years, nearly all America would be Catholic. This is an ideal, it is true, but ideals are goals to be striven for.

In the summer of 1954, the second assembly of the World Council of Churches was held in Evanston, Illinois. Before this event, Samuel Cardinal Stritch of Chicago wrote a letter to the faithful urging them to pray for those outside the fold to become Catholics, for this is the only plan of Christian Unity as envisaged by the Church.

The Cardinal stated clearly that the Church does not take part in such discussions as the Evanston Conference. "They talk about setting up and establishing a Christian Unity, or as they say, a unity of Christian action . . . They gather in international organizations, they hold congresses, conventions and assemblies . . . The Catholic Church does not take part in these organizations or in their assemblies or conferences. She does not enter into any organization in which the delegates of many sects sit down in council or conference as equals to discuss the nature of her unity . . . or to formulate a program of united Christian action." The Church cannot take part in any meeting or group that implies or seems to imply that the Church is searching for a unity that has never been realized or will be realized in the future. The Church holds that she is essentially the same today in doctrine and moral teaching as in the days of Christ and the Apostles.

The prelate then exhorted the faithful to pray for all sincere people separated from the Church. "Pray that they, with God's grace, may find the Church of Christ, the Mother Church that waits for them with open arms and longs to receive them. Pray that they may come to look upon Mary, the Mother of Jesus, as their own true Mother. Pray that, like the Magi of old, they may be given the star of faith to find 'the Child with Mary His Mother' . . . In this Marian year when you are fervently praying to Our Blessed Lady, the Mother of God, remember your brothers and ask our Blessed Lady to bring them into the unity of the Church."

It is not in the spirit of arrogance or pride that such a remark is made, but with a deep realization of the oneness of divine truth and the duty of allegiance to it.

There is no national shrine to Mary in the United States that draws the faithful and touches the hearts of non-Catholics as Lourdes, Fatima, or Guadelupe. Our many beautiful churches and cathedrals do not have the appeal of some of the world famous monuments of devotion, but surely the completion of the great church of the Immaculate Conception in Washington, D.C., has brought many blessings from heaven and will bring the influence of Mary into the lives of many Americans. For Mary is the Lady conquering with love, the woman clothed with the sun who will persuade, and win over all her children, even those who do not as yet love and venerate her.

In times past many tributes were accorded the Virgin Mother of God even by those not of the faith. William Wordsworth (1770-1850) could open his lines of appreciation and admiration in "The Virgin":

Mother! Whose virgin bosom was uncrost
With the least shade of thought to sin allied;
Woman above all women glorified . . .

Henry Adams (1838-1919) could write a "Prayer to the Virgin of Chartres" calling her "Gracious Lady" and protest his undying devotion to the Queen of Heaven:

But years, or ages, or eternity
    Will find me in thought before your throne,
Pondering the mystery of Maternity,
    Soul within Soul—Mother and Child in One!

Such thoughts are not so prevalent among our separated brethren today, though the well-known actress, Cornelia Otis Skinner, could call on Our Lady in these stirring lines:

Mary, most serenely fair
Hear an unbeliever's prayer.
Nurtured in an austere creed
Sweetest Lady, she has need
Of the solace of your grace;
See the tears that stain her face
As she kneels to beg your love—
You whom no one told her of.

Mary is a person who cannot be ignored. Men may scorn her; her erring sons and daughters may reject her; but they cannot be indifferent, because her Mother's love is too great and too strong to be passed by.

It is our hope that Catholic devotion to the Mother of God will be a powerful means of grace for the people of our beloved country. What Fr. Xavier McLeod wrote a century ago should pertain even more today:

"We are prepared to believe that there is no old Catholic country of Europe, there never has been a country in which reverent love and heartfelt devotion for the Blessed Mother of God was more deeply rooted, more ardently cherished, or more fervently and fruitfully practiced than North America. It is unobtrusive but it is real. It guides and influences the hearts of men and it is found pure and glowing. . . ."

May Mary's hour come as it did in Cana in Galilee when she whispered to her Son "They have no wine;" and through the graces from heaven which she dispenses to men, souls may be changed from the pale water of foolish living to the purest wine of love for God and devotion to

His holy Mother. In the Apocalypse St. John could pray: "Come, Lord Jesus." So we pray to Mary: "Come, dear Mother, take over and influence the souls of all men who are your children, even though as yet many do not know you."

6. *The restoration of lapsed Catholics to the sacramental life of the Church.*

This intention has a note of urgency and pity in it. Souls now fallen from God's grace and in sin were once born into supernatural life. They were once living members of Christ's Mystical Body, who knew the divine power and love of God through the sacraments, especially the Eucharist, and were quickened by the inspiration of the Holy Spirit in Confirmation. Once they loved their Mother Mary as devoted children and offered her their Aves and hymns with devotion and confidence.

But now all that is past. Once heirs of paradise, they have forsaken their destiny for "the mess of pottage" of personal ambition, material success, of the involvement of an unlawful marriage. But just as the Divine Shepherd seeks for those who are lost, so His Holy Mother, the Divine Shepherdess, by her prayers and love seeks for those who have separated themselves from the Church. Mary longs for their return, she seeks once again to welcome and meet them in their true home.

The number of those who have lapsed from the Church is staggering. Among the forty-five million Catholics in the United States almost twenty per cent do not attend Sunday Mass regularly. To this number add the thirty-forty per cent in some areas in England, the vast populations in so-called Catholic countries in Europe and nations in South America where the ratio is even higher, and you get some idea of the astounding number of those who have fallen away from the faith or who are very careless in their profession of it. Moreover, this estimate of attendance at Sunday Mass is only one way to gauge the number of lapsed Catholics. Others have cut themselves off from the source of spiritual life through ignorance, neglect, a bad marriage, or a mixed marriage. All over the world it is the same story: in Europe, in Asia, in the Philippines, in Africa. In South America fifty thousand priests are needed at this very hour to restore souls to the faith who have been for years without the sacraments.

These great multitudes of the lapsed are not behind the Iron and Bamboo Curtains, nor in cities and towns held fast by the iron fist of Communism; they are here in our own nation and in other countries where Catholics are free to practice the faith. These people who have lapsed are spiritually dead; they have turned aside from the holy faith, from the Eucharist and the Mass, the value of which even a Protestant writer recognized: "If indeed the Incarnation be the one divine element to which the whole creation moves, the miracle of the altar may well seem to be its restful shadow cast over a dry and thirsty land for the help of man . . . It is the Mass that matters; it is the Mass that makes the difference." But the lapsed Catholic does not realize this truth.

To have become a Catholic and then to have fallen away is immeasurably worse than never becoming a Catholic. We cannot judge those who have sold the pearl of great price, the Catholic faith, for a mere pittance, and we are acutely aware that were it not for God's grace, we might be in a similar plight. But we should do all we can to win these prodigals back to the Church. Indifference, neglect, and even apostasy will give way before the power, the zeal, and the prayer of Our Lady.

It is pitiable that many Catholics do not interest themselves in those who have fallen away. They should recall the parable of the Good Shepherd: "There is more joy in heaven over one sinner who does penance than over ninty-nine who need not penance." They should pray to Our Lady and remember that she is the Divine Shepherdess, brooding over the world, seeking the souls marked with the sacraments of her Son but separated from the One Fold by their own choice.

How many people have returned to the practice of their faith by the persistent devotion of a good mother, a faithful wife, a fervent religious, a priest? How many others have come back, after years of separation, because they were casually faithful to some little practice of devotion to the Mother of God? Their number is legion and only the angels of heaven can record them. Every soul that returns in repentance to God, every heart stung by remorse, every shoulder bowed in sorrow, is a constant memorial to the mother love of the Virgin Mary.

On March 10, 1955, Pope Pius XII gave an address to the pastors and Lenten preachers of Rome and spoke of the necessity of "enlisting the help of an ardent and willing legion of militant Catholics, qualified to spread the teaching and example of Jesus in places where it is almost impossible for the priest to penetrate". For, he continued, there is "so much ground to plough, so many fields to be cultivated, and so many crops to harvest that all the faithful must be apostolic and persevering in their zeal."

The Legion of Mary is perhaps one of the most apostolic movements for the laity in modern times. And its potential is only beginning. Thousands of people have returned to the faith through the zeal and love of apostolic laity, imbued with the love of Mary and the desire to spread her rule over the souls of men.

While all men are loved by Our Lady, those marked with the sign of the faith through the sacraments are the special object of her love. They are like citizens in a strange land who cannot become members of another nation. They are spiritual D.P.'s, destined to become citizens of heaven, marked with the seal of its citizenship, but they will not gain it until they return to the One Shepherd who seeks His sheep and to the One Fold over which Our Lady exercises her profound love.

There is a story told of Mary's influence over a "straying child". It is typical and beautiful. A priest was called to the slum section of an eastern city to minister to a dying woman. Dirty-faced urchins met him on the sidewalk and led him to the dark cellar of a foul-smelling tenement. There beside the furnace, in a welter of soiled underwear, empty liquor bottles, and cigarette butts, on a rusty cot, wrapped in a man's overcoat, lay the dying person.

She groaned with intense pain. The eldest child, a girl of eleven years, said quietly: "Here's a priest to see you."

The woman turned and screamed: "Get out of here!" and she spat at him.

Then someone dragged over an empty beer case and the priest sat beside the cot. He spoke kindly to the poor soul, reminding her that she was dying and that it was time for her to make her peace with God. She continued to call him the foulest names. Then the priest knelt and began to recite the rosary. At first, it was an odd combination of prayer and blasphemy, but as the Aves continued, the woman became silent; tears filled her blood-shot eyes.

As she later said, when the priest prayed the rosary, memories of the past came back to her—memories of her girlhood in the Midwest, of her mother and father, brothers and sisters . . . of herself . . . all kneeling around the dining room table saying the rosary before a little Mary shrine of Our Lady with a candle burning before it. She had been so good then; she was so evil now. But as the last decade began in this unkempt cellar, she answered in words that were so wonderfully real: "Holy Mary, Mother of God, pray for us sinners now and at the hour of our death." She made her confession, received the Eucharist and Extreme Unction, and died peacefully.

Our Lady had won again. So will she intercede for all the spiritually displaced of the world that "they may be one" in the only Fold of the Redeemer of the world. It is the duty of the laity to pray and work with Our Lady for their less fortunate brothers and sisters, separated from the Church by weakness and ignorance.

7. *That the Jewish people come into their inheritance in Jesus Christ.*

The "homecoming" of the Jewish people to the One Fold of Christ is also a special prayer of Our Lady, for she, no less than her divine Son, was a member of this race. She knew the hopes and desires of her people, their longing for the Saviour who would fulfill their expectations and lead them to victory over their enemies. But Mary's soul was pained with grief when they rejected Jesus, so completely and finally, that He died upon a criminal's cross.

But not all turned away from His teaching and His love. The Apostles, the disciples, and many of the first Christians came from this race to whom was entrusted the first deposit of divine revelation. The fairest flower of all— the Lily of Israel, the Rose of Sharon and the Beauty of Carmel, immeasurably greater than Esther or Ruth or Judith —Mary, pleads that her people come to the fulness of truth found only in the Church of Her Son and Saviour.

A poignant scene from the Gospels shows Mary and Joseph seeking their lost Son who had been left behind when they began their trip home from Jerusalem. Both thought the Child was traveling with the other or with relatives. But later the tragic realization that He was with neither wrung their souls with anguish; they hurried back to the Holy City seeking Him who was their all, in the maze of dark, narrow streets, heedless of fatigue or hunger or any need whatever, except that of finding Jesus.

They found Him on the third day, in the pillared halls of the temple where the teachers sat on low stools and around them gathered the eager listeners. In the center of the group was the Child listening to their remarks and answering questions. Surprised but joyful, Mary asked Him: "Son, why hast Thou done so to us? Behold, Thy father and I have sought Thee sorrowing."

It was the grief of a mother's heart. "I have sought Thee sorrowing," she cried. How aptly her words apply to the members of Jesus' race scattered throughout the world.

Mary's anxious heart seeks for all who are her descendants according to the flesh. For if St. Paul could write words of burning love for his brethren outside the Church, how much more does Mary's love embrace these same people, dispersed all over the world.

The Old Testament furnishes us with many noble figures as types of Mary. There was Rachel suffering when she bore her younger son; Miriam guarding the childhood of Moses; Judith saving her people from destruction; Ruth the Moabite who lived a thousand years before Christ, a pagan who became one of Israel's greatest saints, and who vowed her devotion and love to her mother-in-law: "Wherever you go I will go, wherever you lodge I will lodge, your people shall be my people and your God my God." (Ruth 1:16). Again Mary is like the Maccabean mother who suffered seven deaths with the passing of her seven sons, a figure of the *Mater dolorosa* at the foot of the Cross. Little wonder that Mary must hold a special place in her heart for those who are her sons and daughters according to the flesh.

There is a story told of a Jewish woman who lived in

Vienna. She often visited the Catholic Church nearby, but only because of its works of art. She was especially attracted by a picture of the Sorrowful Mother, and often came to admire it.

During the Nazi reign of terror in 1938 she was seized and forced to work for the Storm Troopers. Locked in a room, she had to scrub floors with lye and steel wool. Soon her hands began to smart and then to bleed; the pain was dreadful. Suddenly she heard a scream such as she had never heard before—it was the cry of a slave for freedom. At once she understood the image of the Sorrowful Mother and the words burned in her heart: "I have sought thee sorrowing." She saw that in all men who are united to Christ, His life and Passion are repeated again and again so that all suffering borne for love makes the soul like Him and serves the cause of His redemption. The woman's hands were crimson with blood, but her heart beat with intense joy. Grace had struck with telling force. The next day, she went to the Church of the Sorrowful Mother and asked to become a Catholic.

The same glorious Mother of God, who stood by the Cross of her dying Son, intercedes in heaven for the religious unity of all men; she gives hope and courage to the entire world. Mary worked a miracle with blinding force upon the young Jew, Alphonse Ratisbonne, in the Church of Santa Andrea della Fratte in Rome on January 20, 1842, and brought him to his knees, to the Church, and to the priesthood of Jesus. Her power is not less effective with others of his race.

Another beautiful story in recent times comes from France. It is in letter form:

Most Holy Virgin, I am a Jew. A former deportee, I endured three years suffering in different camps and was one of a convoy of five hundred Jews proceed-

123

ing Hazebrouck, when by the grace of God, I had a chance to escape. Immediately after that I met an abbe. Trembling with fear and covered with filth and grime after six days in a cattle truck, I confronted the priest and told him my story.

The brave priest hid me in his church, fed me, gave me his clothes, and directed me to Lille, to a place where I was safe.

I now wish to thank the Blessed Virgin for my safety and ask a blessing for the abbe who saved my life.

Michel.

This message to Our Lady was tied to the railing of the Grotto of Lourdes during the pilgrimage made to the shrine by many ex-prisoners. It is a striking illustration of how concerned Mary is for the people of her race; it is a simple tribute by one who learned the protective love of her holy Mother and came to the feet of Mary's Son in adoration and humility.

In the plan of Divine Providence the efforts of men can serve the purposes of Almighty God. Thus, the creation of the State of Israel has brought on new problems, but it also has broken down barriers of prejudice and misinformation that have grown up for centuries. Israel is in a state of unrest, but in this condition many are turning away from the religion of the past and to the true faith. Within the past several years more converts were made to the Catholic faith in Israel than had been made in that area for generations.

There are about twelve million Jews in the world, half of them in the United States, and more in New York City than in the State of Israel. Hitler killed more than six million of them, but he did not kill their spirit. They are divided into four groups: the *Indifferents,* who have completely or almost completely thrown off the yoke of religion;

the *Liberals,* who have lightened the burden by introducing changes in the traditional faith; the *Orthodox,* who held to the teachings and practices of the past; and the *Conservatives,* who try to harmonize progress with traditional beliefs.

It is true that many Jewish people have a dislike for the Church, although they look upon the Christians as preparing the way for the Messiah and making known the knowledge of God. As for Our Lord Whom they previously castigated with many denunciations, many rabbis now regard Him as one of the greatest doctors of Israel. Some have even advocated an acceptance of His teachings and the study of His life.

Through the intercession of Our Lady, the Jewish people will come to the true faith. And when that time comes "an insatiable thirst for the apostolate will take hold of the reborn Israel, as it did of the greatest saints and purest children, giving no rest to its spirit nor its body, to its intercession of labor, so long as there remains on earth a soul closed to the holy inebriation of the Cross, or some forgotten or forsaken sheep to be led to its Shepherd". (Msgr. Journet).

These words are true, not because of any promise by man, but by virtue of the inspired word of God. St. Paul uttered words of prophesy which give us certainty and hope for the future: "I would not have you ignorant, brethren, of this mystery (lest you should be wise in your deceits) that blindness in part has happened to Israel, until the fullness of the gentiles should come in, and so all Israel be saved, as it is written:

There shall come out of Sion He that shall deliver
And shall turn away ungodliness from Jacob,
And this is to them my covenant,
When I shall take away their sins.

125

"As concerning the Gospel, indeed, they are enemies for your sake: but as touching the election, they are most dear for the sake of the fathers. For the gifts and calling of God are without repentance." (Rom. 11:25-9).

And Our Lady of the Atonement, Lily of Israel, will welcome her children home.

8. *The missionary extension of Christ's kingdom throughout the World.*

This last intention of prayers and sacrifices for souls is most comprehensive. It includes vast numbers of people, almost countless in extent, six hundred million in China, four hundred and fifty million in India, ninety million in Japan, and many millions in the emerging nations of Africa. We pray that through God's mercy and the intercession of the Mother of God, all of them will come to the true faith.

Mary is Queen of the world as Christ is its King. Mary must reign over the souls of men; nothing must be excluded from her empire. For as Pope Pius XII stated: "Mary's queenship is as vast as the kingdom of her Son: He the Son of God, reflects on His Heavenly Mother the glory, majesty, and dominion of His Kingship for, having been associated with the King of Martyrs in the ineffable work of human redemption as Mother and Cooperatrix, she remains ever associated with Him, with an almost unlimited power, in the disposition of graces which flow from the redemption. Jesus is King throughout all eternity by nature and right of conquest; through Him, with Him, and subordinate to Him, Mary is Queen by grace, by divine relationship, by right of conquest, and singular election. And her kingdom is as vast as that of her Son and God, since nothing is excluded from her dominion."

But when we realize the vast millions of souls who have absolutely no contact with Christianity, even its most distorted forms, who do not know of the Gospel of Christ and the mother-love of Our Lady, we may be appalled at the possibility of their becoming members of the one Church. It seems so impossible. "But grace can where nature cannot", we say, and Mary is a formidable power in God's plan of salvation. She is the strong and conquering woman, foreseen in the garden of Eden as the one who would crush the serpent's head.

For the conquest by Christ of the paganism that hold men captive, we need to enlist the power of Mary. In words adopted from the Mass for the Propagation of the Faith, we pray: "O Mother, who willest that all men should be saved and come to the knowledge of the truth, send, we beseech thee, laborers into the harvest fields of thy Son; grant them to speak the truth with all confidence, that the message of God may spread and be made known and that all peoples may know thee and thy Son . . ."

Missioners in foreign lands report a sincere devotion of many non-Catholic peoples to the Mother of God. Perhaps in the Providence of God this respect for Mary will be the bridge that will lead them to the Church of Christ. For example, at the boundaries of Nepal, three thousand Hindus and Moslems joined three hundred Catholics to honor the Pilgrim Statue of Our Lady of Fatima, as four elephants carried the statue to the Church for rosary and benediction of the Most Blessed Sacrament.

At Rajkot, where there are practically no Catholics, unbelieving ministers of the state and other officials came to venerate the statue. The mayor of Nadiad read a speech of welcome and declared how proud he was to be present on such an occasion. For twelve hours the crowds passed through the church, crowds that were nearly all non-Christian. One old Indian woman expressed the truth simply: "She has shown us that your religion is true. It is not like ours: your religion is a religion of love; ours is one of fear."

The passing of the Pilgrim Statue through other parts of India was like a march of triumph. At Patna, the Brahman governor visited the Catholic Church and prayed before the statue. In the tiny village of Kesra Mec more than twenty-five thousand people came to see the statue; the Rajah sent two hundred and fifty rupees, and his wife sent a petition for prayers. In other regions of India and in Africa as well, Moslems crowded the churches to render homage to the Mother of God. India has its own Lourdes at Perambur (Madras). Other shrines to Mary, well-known to Catholics, Hindus and Moslems alike, are Our Lady of Bandel, Our Lady of Nokamek, and Our Lady of Valienkanni.

Islam does not ignore Our Lady. In the Koran, the Moslem scripture, there are several passages about her. It is said that the Moslems believe in the Immaculate Conception and the Virgin Birth; it is a fact that there are verses on the Annunciation, the Visitation, and the Nativity of Our Lord. Angels are shown accompanying the Blessed Virgin and saying: "O Mary, God has chosen you and purified you, and elected you above all women on earth."

Islam is becoming weaker in northern Africa. The young people of today are beginning to revolt against thirteen centuries of slavery. Morocco, Algeria, Tunisia and other regions are in political and social ferment. Ideas and concepts of the modern world have pierced through the once-impenetrable barrier to find acceptance in the souls of many Moslems.

The danger of political, social and economic revolution is very real. But just as real is the religious force that is invading these areas. The rural areas are becoming mechanized, the cities are booming with industry and a new order has taken possession of people's souls. And the people are potential Catholics—or Communists.

They have come to see that the Koran way of life is not the answer to their problems, and that their sacred book contains many contradictions. And out of their groping for salvation, we pray that they may search for the light, and that they may come upon it.

We pray not only for the Moslems of Africa, but all over the world, for the pagans of Burma, China, Japan, India and the smaller countries, that they may come to the light that is Christ, brought to Him by the soft glow of her who is likened to the moon—Mary, His Mother and theirs.

The Chinese people have a legend about Kwan-yin, the Goddess of Mercy; the Japanese venerate Kwanon; in Africa, the Queen Mother exercises an important role in tribal justice.

And we could make a survey among other peoples and times and find a similar yearning for the ideal Mother. Through the mists of the centuries, embedded in fable and folklore, entwined in the longings and desires of men hidden in the recesses of their souls, is the vision of the Madonna, the Mother of God. These souls, blinded by the ignorance and error into which they have been born, do not know that they seek the Mother of God. However, some day, when her holy image is placed before them and the story of her purity and her love is told to them by a zealous missionary, they too will cry out with joy and love: "This is she whom we long to know. This is the Mother of God; this is our Holy Mother too."

Let us not underestimate the power of Our Lady. She can overthrow a thousand evil spirits; she can subdue all the legions of hell. Mary is the Mother of all men and she is the Star of the Pagans, the star that leads them to Christ. "Mary is the bright and incomparable star, whom we need to see raised above this vast sea, by her merits and giving us light by her example. She is the noble star whose rays illumine the whole world, whose splendor shines in the heavens, penetrates into the depths, and traversing the whole earth, gives warmth rather to souls than to bodies, nourishing virtue, withering vices." (St. Bernard).

Mary is also the star of the pagans who throng our cities, of the vast millions more engrossed in the paganism of worldly pleasure than the tribes of Australia or the bushlands of Africa. But Mary can win these souls, too; she can draw them to Christ. We know that Mary must triumph and that her hour is coming. In the words of the poet, we pray:

> Seraph of heaven! too gentle to be human,
> Veiling beneath that radiant form of Woman
> All that is insupportable in thee
> Of Light, and love and immortality!
> Sweet Benediction in the eternal curse!
> Veiled Glory of this lampless universe!
> Thou Moon beyond the clouds! Thou living Form
> Among the dead! Thou Star above the storm!
>
> (Shelley)

We pray to Our Blessed Lady, Mother of God and Mother of all men, to grant the grace of religious unity to all mankind. Mary is the great means of such unity, for through her the Son of God came to earth and united to Himself all redeemed humanity; through her, men make their approach to God and achieve unity with Him. Religious unity is a gigantic enterprise, staggering and overwhelming in its proportions, but it can be accomplished through the power, the love, and the influence of her whom God loves so much. We pray that Mary, the *Conquistadora*, the Conqueress, as the Spanish people love to call her, will share in and bring about the conquest of the world for Christ the King, and that she will truly be the Queen of the Universe.

We do not know when this religious unity for all men

will be attained, but we may be certain that it will come. For the Woman mentioned in the first book of the Bible, Genesis, as conquering the serpent, is also the Woman clothed with the sun in the final book of the Bible, the Apocalypse. From the first book of the Bible to the last, Mary is the Mighty Lady. She is foreshadowed in her daughters in the Old Testament; she comes forth briefly but strikingly in the New Testament, always with her Son. As time moves on and the world grows old, the beauty and influence of Mary, the Mother of God, becomes ever more evident. The prayer of Christ for Unity will be fulfilled, in answer to a tremendous chorus of petition and love and confidence rising up to heaven: "That all may be one". This plea will be answered through the Virgin Mary, all-holy Mother of God. For she is Our Lady of the At-one-ment, Our Lady of Unity.

Six ❧ Our Lady of the At-one-ment

"Our mission is to extend devotion to Our Lady of the Atonement throughout the whole world."   —Father Paul.

The Franciscan Order has always been noted for its love of the Virgin Mother of God. The Little Poor Man of Assisi made Our Lady the patroness of his whole apostolic venture and consecrated himself and his Order to her. He made the tiny chapel of St. Mary of the Angels the cradle and the mother church of the Order. His beloved poverty was "the queen of virtues because it sparkled with such brilliance in the King of Kings and in His Queenly Mother." His earliest biographer, Celano, tells us that Francis "sought unceasingly to render homage and praise to the Mother of Christ. At her feet he poured out a stream of fervent prayer and offered her transports of love so intense and so perfect that they went beyond all human language. His hours of sleep were few; for the most part he spent the night in prayer, praising God and His glorious Virgin Mother."

In the office of the Passion, composed in honor of "the beloved Son who was born of the Virgin Mary," St. Francis began and concluded each hour with this beautiful tribute: "Holy Virgin Mary, there was never anyone like you born in the world among women! Daughter and hand-maid of the Most High King, Our Father in heaven. Mother of the most holy Lord Jesus Christ. Spouse of the Holy Ghost! With the archangel St. Michael, and all the virtues of heaven, and all the saints, pray for us at the throne of your beloved most holy Son, Our Lord and Master."

This same spirit of complete dedication to Our Lady has lived in the hearts of all devoted sons of Francis for seven centuries. St. Anthony of Padua preached her praises to the thousands who gathered on the French and Italian hillsides, St. Bonaventure wrote magnificent treatises in her honor, while John Duns Scotus became the champion of Her Immaculate Conception, and the new doctor of the Church, St. Lawrence of Brindisi, penned his mighty volume, the *Mariale*. Maximillian Kolbe, who died a martyr's death in a concentration camp in our own day, wrought wonders of grace through his all-embracing love of the Virgin Imma-culate.

Preparing the Way.

In the twentieth century, with its almost miraculous advance in technical progress, its global conflicts which have scarred whole nations, its struggle against atheistic communism, another Friar has come upon the stage of the Church's history and has taken his place in the annals of the Franciscan Order. His life was unusual, but so too were his loyalty to the Church and his burning love for the Mother of God. Father Paul, S.A., the founder of the Society of the Atonement, has often been called a modern Apostle of Unity, Father of the Poor, and Friend of Missionaries over all the world. But another claim to glory rests securely upon his exceptional devotion to the Blessed Virgin, whom he honored with the new and distinctive title of Our Lady of the Atonement.

Even during his non-Catholic years, Father Paul displayed a special love for the Queen of heaven and earth. He began the erection of his first small friary at Graymoor on September 8, 1900, the feast of the Nativity of Our Lady, and had it dedicated on the feast of the Immaculate Conception, December 8th.

With Mother Lurana Mary Francis, S.A., the foundress of the Atonement Sisters, he began the Rosary League of Our Lady of the Atonement in 1901 and published the monthly *Rose Leaves* to promote devotion to Mary under the new title. Father Paul prayed her rosary often, he preached her glories, especially that of the Immaculate Conception, and he loved her feast days. And when almost all pulpits were closed to him because of his views on Christian Unity, so that he was forced to inaugurate the publication of *The Lamp*, he entrusted this project to the care of the Virgin Mother of God. In the first issue, February, 1903, he wrote: "We place *The Lamp* under the special protection and patronage of Our Immaculate Lady Mary, Queen of Heaven, and her Seraphic Knight, St. Francis of Assisi. Candelmas, the beautiful feast of the Purification, when she who was 'The Lamp of Burnished Gold' came into the temple bearing the Light of the World, marks the first appearance of *The Lamp*. We have lighted it as a witness to the Old Faith as taught by the English Church before a wicked king severed her from the Center of Unity."

Frequently *The Lamp* carried articles on Our Lady, often reprinted from Catholic publications and always reflecting the mind of the editor. When Father Paul wrote a study on the primacy of the Pope, *The Prince of the Apostles*, in collaboration with the Rev. Spencer Jones, he devoted the last chapter to Papal Infallibility and the Immaculate Conception. He quoted with approval from Bishop Ullathorne: "Soon after St. Bonaventure there arose in his order the famous John Duns Scotus, who first at Oxford and then in a disputation before the University of Paris, laid the foundation for the true doctrine so solidly, and dispelled the objections in a manner so satisfactory, that from that moment it prevailed. It was Scotus who removed the great objection of St. Thomas. He proved that so far from being excluded from redemption, the Blessed Virgin obtained from her divine Son the greatest of graces and her redemption, through that mystery of her immaculate preservation from sin. And from this time the doctrine of the Immaculate Conception not only gained a vast deal of ground in the schools of the Universities, and became the common opinion there, but the Immaculate Conception came to be established in Rome..."

On another occasion the Graymoor Founder strongly defended devotion to Our Lady and to the Rosary. "There is no lie forged in hell," he wrote in *The Lamp*, "more in conflict with the will of God expressed in Scripture and Catholic tradition, than the Protestant conceit that they honor Christ best who most ignore the existence of His Mother. 'What God hath joined together let no man put asunder,' and there is no divorce more horrible as a flagrant violation of the fiat of Almighty God than the divorce made by Protestant reformers between Christ and the Blessed Virgin. The fruit of such violence to revealed truth must of necessity be all sorts and kinds of heresy and goes far to explain the skepticism and unbelief which honeycombs the Church of England today."

"If we accept the witness of the Catholic Church in regard to other matters of faith," he continued, "there can be no valid reason for rejecting what she bids us believe about the efficacy of prayer addressed to Our Lady and Mother in Heaven. There is no better way to realize the truth of the Catholic Religion all the way through than to practice it, and if our Anglican brethren would know for themselves the reality of Mary's love for them personally and her readiness to help and intercede with God on their behalf, let them test it by calling upon her devoutly in every hour of need and just take it for granted that the Catholic Church knows what she is talking about when she affirms and reiterates, so continually, that Christ in addressing St. John at the foot of the Cross, in reality addressed us all, saying 'behold thy Mother,' and that having constituted her the Universal Mother of the redeemed, Almighty God has qualified her for her office by assuming her into heaven, enthroning her at the right hand of Jesus Christ, her Son, and giving her command over a great retinue of ministering spirits to do her bidding in ministering to those who look up to her from every part of our far-off world and who never cease to cry: 'Holy, Mary, Mother of God, pray for us sinners now and at the hour of our death.' (Aug. 1905)

Father Paul had testified to his love for Mary by celebrating the golden jubilee of the definition of the dogma of the Immaculate Conception in 1904, and by devoting an issue of *The Lamp* to "The Immaculate Conception and Church Unity." He was especially grateful that his friary had been dedicated on the feast of the Immaculate Conception in 1900, and that Foundation Day for the Society of the Atonement was December 15, 1898, then kept as the Octave of the Immaculate Conception, and now the feast of Mary, Queen of the Franciscan Order.

But if Father Paul's devotion to Our Lady was prominent as a non-Catholic, it blossomed forth in his Catholic years, after the reception of the Society of the Atonement into the Catholic Church on October 30, 1909. He never wearied of promoting the Rosary League of Our Lady of the Atonement and of asking the faithful to wear the Atonement medal in honor of Our Lady. He believed his Society was raised up by God to promote devotion to Our Lady under the title of the Atonement.

The first writing on Our Lady of the Atonement appeared in *Rose Leaves,* October, 1901. It is a fine synthesis of the Atonement idea: Mary on Calvary and the Mother of Unity. It is a fitting appraisal from the pen of Graymoor's founder, he for nearly forty years who would use the press, the radio, and the pulpit to make known the glories of our Atonement Mother.

Our Lady of the Atonement

The Blessed Virgin is known among Catholics by many names and invoked under many titles. Famous among these are the following: Our Lady of Grace, Our Lady of Victory, Our Lady of Good Counsel, Our Lady of Sorrows, Our Lady of Mercy. In her wonderful condescension and love the Mother of God has been pleased to reveal herself to the Children of the Atonement under a new name, thus giving remarkable evidence that the honor, love and prayers to her as *OUR LADY OF THE ATONEMENT* she is graciously pleased to accept. We have every reason to believe that the Blessed Virgin especially loves this title that links her name with that of Jesus in the glorious work of the Atonement wrought upon the Cross. It must bring to her remembrance that blessed Atonement Day when she stood by the Cross of Jesus and heard Him say to her: "Woman behold thy son," and to the Disciple whom He loved: "Behold thy Mother." Then too, Atonement speaks of reconciliation, pardon, peace, of the fulfillment of the prayer, first breathed by her Divine Son, so often repeated by herself, that Christian believers might be One.

Can we invoke the Blessed Virgin with a title more apt to touch her maternal heart than the one which associates her with Calvary's sacrifice and proclaims her the compassionate Mother of us poor sinners, redeemed by the Precious Blood of Jesus?

Hail Mary of the Atonement, my Lord's Mother and mine, pray for me and all who thus invoke thee now and at the hour of our death. Amen.

In the following pages we shall present a summary of Father Paul's teaching on Our Lady of the Atonement from his sermons, radio talks and pages in *The Lamp*. He did not write an *ex professo* treatise on Our Lady of the Atonement, but for many years he presented a fine treatment of the subject for his spiritual sons and daughters. He was the Herald and Knight of Our Lady of the Atonement.

Our Lady of the Atonement, Standing by the Cross

The most obvious truth suggested by the Atonement title is Mary's role in the sacrifice of Calvary, associated with Jesus in the salvation of the world. "The invocation of Our Lady of the Atonement," Father Paul wrote early in his career as a Catholic, "brings home to us the truth that Our Lord Himself here declared. She was one of the elect of God, the elect of the Father; she had been conceived in the mind of God, ages and ages before her creation. St. John, in the vision of the Apocalypse, declares that he saw a vision of the Lamb of God in heaven, slain long before man was created; before the worlds were called into being in the purpose and mind of God, the offering of Christ was preordained, as also the creation of her who was to be the Mother of the Incarnate Word; and when she stands by the Cross, she is there as God's elect. God the Father had so ordained and willed it, and she, by her cooperation with the divine will and her participation in the chalice of Our Lord's suffering and His agony, became our glorious Lady of the Atonement."

Father Paul told his associates in the Society of the Atonement and the members of the Rosary League, that the mystery of Calvary should always be present in their minds and hearts. By virtue of her sacrifice at the foot of the Cross, Mary became the Mother of all the faithful. "You know that the sorrowful mystery of Our Lady standing at the foot of the Cross is the one above all others that members of the Rosary League should meditate upon so as to understand and appreciate how pleasing it must be to the Mother of God to be addressed by the title of Our Lady of the Atonement. Hear Jesus say to her: 'Woman, behold thy son!' and then to St. John, 'Behold thy Mother!' In these words, the Lord of heaven and earth crowns Mary with the Motherhood of all the elect who should be redeemed by His precious, atoning blood, and through St. John, He addressed Himself to all the Children of the Atonement until the end of the world, saying: 'Behold thy Mother!' "

Father Paul explained the importance of this Marian title. For him it was the most beautiful and the most expressive of all, and he sought to share this conviction with others. "It is among the most treasured and sacred traditions of our Institute," he declared, "that it was the Blessed Virgin herself who first taught us to call her by that name and there are cogent reasons why we should give this title a favorite place among the many by which she is invoked." He set forth two reasons why Our Lady must love the name with special affection: (1) because of her role in the mystery of the Atonement, and (2) because it confirms and ratifies her mission as Mother of all men. "First among these reasons must be her own devotion to the mystery of the Atonement, for it was by the death of her Son on the Cross, which cost Him the last drop of His Blood and made her pre-eminently the Mother of Sorrows that the wall of division between God and man was broken down

and both made one (Eph. 2:14) through Christ's Atoning
Sacrifice. As the Blessed Virgin is inseparably associated
with our Divine Redeemer in the mystery of the Incarnation,
so is she closely associated with Him in the great act of
the Atonement. Thus she is always represented in the gospel
and in the liturgy of the Catholic Church as standing by
the Cross when Christ was crucified thereon.

> At the Cross her station keeping.
> Stood the mournful Mother weeping,
> Close to Jesus to the last.

"There is a second reason," he added, "hardly less
weighty than the first why the title, Our Lady of the Atonement should powerfully appeal to the Mother of God. It
was through the Incarnation that she became the New Eve
and Mother of all the regenerate, who being redeemed
by the Precious Blood, are predestined to eternal life as
adopted sons of God and heirs to the kingdom of heaven.
The third time Our Lord spoke on the Cross, it was to
emphasize this phase of the Atonement when He said to
His Mother: 'Behold thy Son' and to St. John: 'Behold thy
Mother'. Thus by virtue of the Atonement, Mary is the
Mother of all who live through Christ."

The Red Mantle

As Our Lady of the Atonement, Mary is always shown
with a red mantle to symbolize the Most Precious Blood of
her Divine Son "when she compassionated with Him in
the great suffering and sacrifices that were necessary to
beget sons of His glory." Father Paul declared that the
connection of the red mantle with the Atonement should
be obvious, "for it was during the shedding of the Most

Precious Blood of her Divine Son, the very blood He had derived from her own Immaculate Heart, that the redemption of the world was wrought and an atonement made for the sins of the world by the Lamb of God. Our Lady of the Atonement stood by the Cross when the Atoning Sacrifice was enacted and it is most fitting that she should wear a red mantle accepting our homage and devotion under the title of Our Lady of the Atonement."

Later this idea was incorporated into the special hymn in honor of Our Lady of the Atonement, written by Brother Philip Ilberry, S.A., about 1920. The third stanza of the hymn is as follows:

Remind us by thy mantle
    All steeped in crimson red
The Precious Blood of Jesus
    To save men's souls was shed;
Remind us of thy sorrow,
    Thy sense of bitter loss
When thou, Atonement Mother,
    Didst stand beneath the Cross.

And the other verses are these:

(1)

Our Lady of the Atonement
    O! show thyself to be
A mother of thy children
    Who have recourse to thee.
Obtain for us dear Mother
    A faith and love sincere;
Midst trials and temptation
    Thy grace to persevere.

141

(2)

From strife and vain contention,
From passion's evil sway,
Our Lady of the Atonement
Protect us day by day.
When earth-born storms fast gather
Around the Church, may He
Hark to thy voice, dear Mother
And send swift help through thee.

(4)

O! when this life is ending
And its last feeble ray
Is fading in the twilight
That comes at close of day,
Then hasten, O dear Mother,
And close our weary eyes
And bear us up rejoicing
With thee to Paradise.

Father Paul spoke of Mary's suffering in union with her Crucified Son. She co-suffered, co-offered and co-satisfied with Him in the Sacrifice of the Cross. She shared formally in His mission and its achievement. "When she saw her Son rejected, cruelly mocked, spit upon, and bearing His heavy Cross to Calvary, and saw Him nailed to the Tree, she herself stood in anguish, her heavy heart beating with His as the Crucified Redeemer of the world." Still, it was by virtue of suffering and sorrow that she acquired her title. "By her cooperation with the divine will and by her participation in the chalice of the Lord's suffering, she became our glorious Lady of the Atonement." Christ was the one Mediator who restored all men to the friendship and love of God. Yet in a secondary and auxiliary role, Mary, His Mother, "was the mediatrix of the human family when she stood at the Cross as Our Lord was lifted up that He might draw all men to Himself."

In a thought similar to that of St. Cyril of Alexandria who said: "Take away Mary and the Cross falls," Father Paul declared: "The slain Victim, taken down from the Cross, is laid in the arms of His Mother all covered with His Own Blood and that Blood stains the garments of the Blessed Virgin. How impossible to disassociate either Our Lord or Our Lady from the Precious Blood."

At another time the Poverello of Graymoor presented the thought of Mary's role in the mystery of Calvary in this precise form: "She is necessarily of the Atonement, since it was the will of God that she play a fundamental part in the Atonement or Redemption. This is not to say that without her, man would have remained unredeemed, but that God's plan gave her a large share in the redemptive work. When we address the Blessed Mother as 'of the Atonement', we mean, then, that there is some very close bond between the Atonement and Mary. Although her part is in no way similar in nature to that of her Divine Son, Mary cooperated with Jesus Christ as no other creature did, in His work of reconciling man with God. Her claim to this high title rests most solidly on the fact that she consented to become the Mother of the Redeemer; that she suffered with Jesus during the Passion; and that all graces merited for mankind by Christ have come to us through Mary."

This modern Francis explained Mary's singular appreciation of the mystery of the Cross. By the cross, she too was redeemed; her redemption was a preservation rather than a liberation from sin, according to the famous distinction made by John Duns Scotus. "Just as the sacrifice of the Old Law took sin by anticipation of the sacrifice of the Lamb of God upon Calvary, so it endowed the Blessed

Virgin with the wonderful privilege of being conceived without sin which came to her through the Atoning Sacrifice of the Cross. Consequently, she must have a keen appreciation of her dignity and glory as 'blessed among women' and she must have a tremendous respect and affection for the Atonement of Calvary because it means so much to her."

During the monthly novena to Our Lady of the Atonement, Father Paul requested his followers to meditate on the meaning of the Atonement and be inspired with a deeper devotion, not only toward Mary, but her Divine Son. "On the Cross, we know Our Lord spoke to Our Lady of the Atonement and said: 'Behold thy Son' and to the typical son of the Atonement, he said: 'Behold thy Mother'. So there is a very real way in which we can look up to that Mother, bless her and love her for the great gift to us, the gift of her Child, not only to die for us, but to live for us and in us, so that we might say with St. Paul: 'It is no longer that I live, but Christ lives in me'. Our hearts go out, therefore, in deepest gratitude and love to Mary for the great and unspeakable gift of her Son to us, even as Christ, the Son, in His death upon the Cross, gave her to us to be our Mother."

The sons of Mary should be "heralds of Christ", loving with His love and manifesting the spirit of the Gospel to men, for Jesus has given us "a commission to represent Him to the world and to carry on His ministry". He urged his Friars to be "dutiful and holy", and make Christ known to the world. If they do so, "Our Lady will look down and see the image of Christ . . . stamped upon them and she will take delight" in them because they perpetuate the work of her Son in saving souls.

Father Paul asserted that the children of Our Lady must expect to suffer even as she did and to share in the mystery of the Saviour's Cross. The disciple is not above the Master, and the child is not above his Mother. "This Mother of the Atonement is marked with the Passion of Christ as are all the children that reign with him in glory ... All of them must, in some form or other, drink of the chalice of the Lord's Passion and be associated with Him in His battle and struggle for the redemption of mankind."

He said that Our Lady watches over the faithful in their bearing the Cross and in their war against the powers of darkness: "... looking down upon them is Our Lady of the Atonement, Our Lady of the Red Mantle, the Mediatrix who suffered with Our Lord upon the Cross as He was transfixed with the nails in His hands and feet. For even as she brought Him as a child into the temple to present Him to God with all the joy and gladness of a Mother's love, even as she was told by the prophecy of Simeon that a sword should pierce her heart, so as children of the Atonement we must realize that we are called in some degree or another to enter into the suffering of Christ and into the sufferings of His Mother, for Our Lord said: "Except a man take up his cross and deny himself he cannot be my disciple."

Father Paul called attention to Mary's right to freedom from suffering because of the absence of original sin, but actually she did suffer, innocent as she was, with Christ, "on account of the sins of others and seeing the sorrow of her Son" when men would not listen to His teaching and when they crucified Him and put Him to death. "So we must realize that we must, in some measure, be willing to share in Our Lord's chalice of suffering and one of the greatest consolations to us is the invocation of Our Lady of the Atonement, or Our Lady of the Red Mantle." But the crown of glory will come through the mediation of Our Atonement Mother..." because we have tasted of the suffering and anguish of Christ and found the struggle and battle of this world to be good and holy and have resisted the powers of darkness in the spiritual combat, we shall be crowned in heaven, and all this will be the triumph of grace through the intercession of our glorious Mother, Our Lady of the Atonement."

In a radio talk of 1936, Father Paul explained the place of Mary in the Christian life. He said there is but one Mediator, Christ Himself, who had delegated the exercise of the office to His ministers. "In the same way, when Our Lord said to St. John: 'Behold thy Mother' He gave His Mother, not only to St. John, but to all the faithful down through the Christian centuries, but in giving her that office, He also endowed her with the qualities and the power to prove herself a real Mother." Catholics who use the Hail Mary ask the Blessed Virgin to take up their prayers and address God in their behalf. This "is only putting into practice the very words of Christ when He said: 'Son, behold thy Mother'".

The text of the Apocalypse, "A great sign appeared in the heaven, a woman clothed with the sun," is now used for the Feast of the Assumption. Of the text about the woman with child, pursued by the dragon, Father Paul declared that this is also "Our Lady of the Atonement and the child represents her children of the Cross, those that Christ gave to her, redeemed by His Precious Blood and born again into the kingdom of glory." "Believe me ... we have had quantities of experiences and demonstrations, not only that the Blessed Virgin can hear prayers, but that it is the will of God and of her divine Son that we go to her as our Mother and expect her to give her children that assistance and help which they need."

The Graymoor Founder, like many saints and spiritual writers, explained the miracle of Cana, the changing of the water into wine at the request of Mary, as an example of her power with God. There Our Lady occupied the position "of an advocate, interested in and sympathizing with this

146

young couple in the embarrassment"... As Our Lord is the same yesterday, today and forever, and changes not, so Our Lady, as she stands there on the threshold of the Gospel, as an advocate in heaven, exercising her great power with God on behalf of the distressed and those who have recourse to her in their needs here on earth.

Father Paul taught that Mary is just as interested in people today, in their problems and difficulties, and hears their pleadings. "When we speak of her as our Mother of the Atonement, we think of her standing by the Cross, and there, Our Lord, in the person of St. John, gives her all the redeemed as her children, so that she is the New Eve, the Mother of All who live in Christ. Consequently, she has the Mother-heart and we are her children. When she was at Cana, in Galilee, perhaps this young couple were relatives of hers and she was interested in them as relations; she comes and entreats for them. But we are her children and she loves us as a Mother; she is interested in us as her children. With what confidence ought we to turn to her, knowing that she will be interested and will plead for us in heaven, not just because we are her friends or acquaintances but because we are her children."

Many times Father Paul said that the members of the Society of the Atonement should be "pre-eminent in their devotion to Our Lady of the Atonement." He himself set the example of what the devotion should be by his own childlike, unwavering trust in and love for Mary under the holy name. Firmly convinced that the feast of Our Lady of the Atonement would some day become a universal feast in the Church, he saw his Society with a special mission in regard to her. "The peculiar contribution which the Society of the Atonement is to render to the honor and the devotion of the Blessed Virgin, is that of the Atonement, by and through which we participate in that grace which was given by sharing in Christ's sacrifice on the Cross, to

147

the Blessed Virgin to spare her (from sin) to be His Mother."

On the feast of the Immaculate Conception in 1938, he stated that his followers should promote love for Mary in the Church. It was not enough to love her personally; they must spread this love. "Our Lady manifested herself as our Atonement Mother, and it is not only personally that we should render devotion to her, but we should have great zeal to propagate that devotion throughout the entire length and breadth of the Church Universal." On another occasion he wrote: "Cultivate in your own lives an ever increasing devotion to Our Lady of the Atonement and preach that devotion to others." And again: "As the title must be dear to the Blessed Virgin, so it must be dear to us. So let us spread this devotion, knowing that those who preach her under that invocation will find her especially generous." He stated that the Atonement Religious should be prominent in their devotion to Mary: "Now, if we are well grounded in our faith and have confidence in this title as being given to us by Our Lady herself, it ought to inspire us with an extraordinary devotion to the Mother of God; we should have it in common with all religious, but as Children of the Atonement, we ought to excel in that devotion."

Frequently Father Paul would say that the name Atonement means much to Our Lady and would quote the text from Romans (5:11) of the title: "We joy in God through our Lord Jesus Christ by whom we have received the Atonement." He commented thus: "Although penned by St. Paul under the inspiration of the Holy Ghost, the great apostle himself cannot even now in heaven pronounce these words with such fullness of joy, of love and gratitude as the Blessed Virgin. Consider what the Atonement means to her. The end, or purpose, of Christ's sacrifice of Himself upon the Cross was the reconciliation of man to God and the establishment of a condition of at-one-ment, or one-ness, between the Divine Nature and the human nature which has no equivalent in the relation of God to the angels or any other creature."

The Glory of the Name

As Founder of the Friars and Sisters of the Atonement, Father Paul often spoke of the primacy of the title of Our Lady of the Atonement. In his mind, it was one of the most important and significant in the whole list of titles accorded to the Mother of God and approved by the Church. For the members of his Society it was *the* title above all others by which Mary should be called. " ... when the Blessed Virgin teaches her children under the title of *Our Lady of the Atonement,* even though she be so invoked for the first time in the twentieth century, that title nevertheless is of such importance and intrinsic worth that it cannot take any other than first rank among the modes of address by which the faithful are accustomed to invoke the Queen of heaven and earth."

July 9th, the Feast of Our Lady of the Atonement, is also the anniversary of Father Paul's discovery of the name Atonement at St. John's Church, Kingston, New York, in 1893. He regarded this favor as a very special blessing from God, and in his eyes the Atonement name for Mary was clear indication that this Society was singularly loved by God. "Now it seems to me," he declared, "of divine predilection toward our holy Institute that we are privileged to address the Mother of God by a title that is new and yet as ancient as Christianity. It is a title that has to do with her intimate relationship with the Redeemer of the world as He hung upon the Cross and offered Himself in sacrifice for the sins of the world. ... If we had no other reason for believing that this Society was dear to Our Lord than just that one thing, it would be ample ground for regarding

149

our Society as something more than an ordinary religious foundation."

Father Paul took special joy in the fact that Graymoor added a new title to the glorious array honoring the Mother of God. There are other titles distinctively American (Our Lady of Maryknoll, Our Lady of Washington, Our Lady of the Ozarks), but this is the only title of American origin, at least thus far, that has its own distinctive Office and Mass. "When we study the history of all religious foundations," he said, "we find servants of God, the ones that God has chosen and called for the work of laying some new branch of a religious family, have always been characterized by a special devotion to the Blessed Mother and since the Society of the Atonement, called into being in these latter days, is a Society of God's predilection, it is natural to suppose that it will manifest in some way devotion to the Mother of God. I wonder if we appreciate sufficiently the great mark of predilection that God has put upon it, that He has privileged us to know the Blessed Virgin and to honor her by a so glorious and yet so new a title in the Church, Our Lady of the Atonement, even as the name Society of the Atonement, was preserved through all the centuries that our Institute might hold it in these latter days, although it is so obvious and so prominent that one wonders how it ever could have been preserved." At another time, when speaking on Our Lady of the Atonement (Feast Day, 1925) he said that members of the Society might "rejoice today in the great privilege that is given us to invoke Our Lady by a new title and let us encourage ourselves with the marks of predestination, love and favor which God has bestowed upon this Institute."

For Father Paul, the title of Our Lady of the Atonement was a "major" title. He said that other names such as Our Lady of Peace, Our Lady, Help of Christians, Our Lady, Refuge of Sinners might be considered as of secondary importance, but not Our Lady of the Atonement. It was of primary importance because of Mary's relationship to Christ as Saviour of the world. "The privilege of invoking her by a new title, that of Our Lady of the Atonement, is certainly a tremendous favor, a feast in honor of which has the approval of the Holy Father, the Pope. A wonderful favor indeed to our Holy Society and a mark of its predilection with God. We cannot realize, I am sure, too strongly the fact that the Society of the Atonement is a great creation of God with a tremendous vocation and that it is loved by Our Blessed Mother. We should always, then, have recourse to Our Lady of the Atonement in all our troubles and turn our eyes toward her with the utmost confidence in her love, her maternal watchfulness over us individually and in everything that concerns the well-being of the Society of the Atonement."

Father Paul pointed to Mount Carmel as the place of origin of devotion to Mary under the special title of Queen and Beauty of Carmel. In a similar manner he believed, Graymoor should become prominent by propagating devotion to Our Lady of the Atonement. "We do not doubt," Father Paul said, "that as the Blessed Virgin showed an especial predilection for Mount Carmel, so she chose this mountain (The Mount of the Atonement) long before the coming of the Friars and set her affection upon it as a sacred eminence, where the Atonement of her Divine Son in which she so intimately participated, would be illustrated and magnified in that last days of the world." He called the Mount of the Atonement "an American Carmel."

Father Paul also stated that the title must be especially loved by Mary because it refers to her spiritual Motherhood over all the redeemed: ". . . the Motherhood of Mary, as far as redeemed humanity is concerned, is bound up with the Atonement, and the Blessed Virgin must value it accordingly, and therefore the title, when applied to her, must be exceedingly precious." And again: "When Jesus constituted Our Lady of the Atonement, the Mother of all that should be redeemed by His Precious Blood on Calvary's Cross, He endowed her with the abundant capacity to discharge her function as a Mother, and although her family is so huge and immense and scattered all over the world, God has given her the capacity of mind and heart to think about and watch over all her children, no matter where they are on this earth." Of her spiritual Motherhood he also said: "Not only did Our Lady of the Atonement cooperate with Our Lord by giving Him her Blood for our salvation, she again cooperated in her acceptance of the Sacred Motherhood which He bestowed upon her as she stood by the Cross."

In a conference with his spiritual daughters, the Sisters of the Atonement, he said: "You are working on your missions to make Our Lady known, more and more, by the beautiful title of the Atonement and feel the wonderful confidence in her Mother love towards each and every one of you . . . She must have a very great love for the Institute and therefore the Sisters may always shelter themselves under the mantle of her maternal protection and feel that they will not look and appeal to her in vain."

The importance of the name of Our Lady of the Atonement was further emphasized by Father Paul in a letter to the members of the Rosary League. "Coming into existence nearly seven hundred years after the founding of the Three Orders of St. Francis, the Society of the Atonement, true to the Franciscan tradition, has always manifested a more than ordinary devotion to the Mother of God and certainly the Sons and Daughters of the Atonement have the most powerful reasons for displaying such a devotion, inasmuch as the Mother of God herself conferred upon the Society the very great distinction and honor of invoking her under a title never before bestowed upon her, namely, Our Lady of the Atonement; a title that must henceforth rank among the very foremost in dignity of all those titles which the Church, from time to time, during the long centuries of her history has bestowed upon the Immaculate Virgin. No one will dispute that the Atonement ranks with the Incarnation itself as the two most important and essential factors in the divine economy of man's salvation and when the Blessed Virgin teaches her children to invoke her under the title of Our Lady of the Atonement, even though she be so invoked for the first time in the twentieth century, that title, nevertheless, is of such intrinsic worth that it cannot take any other than first rank among the modes of address by which the faithful are accustomed to invoke the Queen of heaven and earth."

Father Paul expressed the relationship of Our Lady of the Atonement to her children for the month of May: "During this, the month of Mary, the Motherhood of the Blessed Virgin is emphasized, not only because by virtue of the Atonement she is also the New Eve and Mother of that vast multitude which have been regenerated in baptism and born anew into the Kingdom of God. In other words, she is the Mother of us all. Now the Atonement lays special stress on this glorious fact. It was from the altar of His Atoning Sacrifice that Jesus, the New Adam, spoke to Mary, the New Eve, saying 'Woman, behold thy Son!' and to St. John, the ideal Son of the Atonement, 'Son, behold thy Mother!' Therefore in adopting the title, Children of the Atonement, for the members and associates of the Society of the Atonement we are emphasizing a great and wonderful truth—a Child of the Atonement is a Child of God and of Mary, born again of the Holy Ghost, sprinkled with the Precious Blood of the Redemption and destined for citizenship in the heavenly Jerusalem."

Father Paul explained the origin of the term "Children of the Atonement." It was not intended in a restrictive sense, so as to exclude those who were not members or associates of the Society of the Atonement. Rather it was to emphasize in a special way man's "spiritual lineage in Jesus and Mary of the Atonement. In thus calling ourselves Children of the Atonement, we, of course, do not claim a monopoly of the title, as though no others than ourselves were Children of the Atonement, but we use it to bring home to ourselves a livelier realization of the birthright in Mount Calvary and its Cross and our spiritual lineage in Jesus and Mary of the Atonement, even as widespread sodalities of the Children of Mary are meant not to imply that no one else than they who belong to the sodality are Mary's children, but by reason of the sodality and its name they are helped to realize, more vividly, that they are of a truth Children of Mary."

Now we may turn to the second meaning of Our Lady of the Atonement.

Mother of Unity

There is another theological truth contained in the title of Our Lady of the Atonement; it derives from Mary's participation in the mystery of the Cross. It is the concept of Unity—that Our Lady has a part to play in preserving the faithful in the Church and bringing souls to the unity of the Church. Mary is Our Lady of Unity, always praying for the great At-one-ment of men with God.

Often as Father Paul spoke and wrote about Our Lady's share in the mystery of Calvary, he also treated her function in uniting men to Christ. Just as the Mother of God had a special role as companion, helpmate, and co-sufferer with Christ in the mystery of Calvary, so also she exercises a particular mission in the plan of salvation and sanctification, by which the merits of the Atonement are applied to the souls of men. For Father Paul, Our Lady of the Atonement meant Our Lady of Unity, constantly interceding for the conversion of all men separated from her Son. "When, therefore, as children of the Atonement, we address the Blessed Mother under that title, let us think of her as 'Our Lady of Unity', and let us consecrate ourselves afresh at her altar to contribute what lies within our power of prayers, sacrifice and charitable endeavor to bring our separated brethren into the unity of the One Fold under the One Shepherd."

For just as the devil entices a person to commit sin, separating him from Christ, removing the unity of the Redeemer and the soul, so also Satan has brought about schism, heresy and indifferentism by which millions are cut off from full unity with the Saviour and the Church He founded. But Father Paul confidently predicted victory over the powers of hell—victory through Mary. "Satan by fomenting strife and fostering heresy and schism has separated many millions from the unity of the Church . . . but Our Lady of the Atonement will yet crush the serpent's head even where he has, until now achieved his greatest victories." He went on to make this statement: "Through her all-prevailing intercession on the Holy Spirit she will bring about such a world-wide movement of separated Christians to the center of Catholic Unity that the return of the Wandering Sheep to communion with the Apostolic See will far transcend in magnitude and importance the lapse of the Greeks from Unity in the tenth century and the Protestant defection in the sixteenth century combined. We dare to make this prophecy, not because we have the vision of the Seer, but because we believe that God, the Father Almighty, will answer the prayer of His Son, Jesus Christ, and Our Lady of the Atonement will have a leading part in this glorious accomplishment."

Father Paul believed that Mary, as the New Eve, the Mother of all the living in the mystical Body of Christ, would have a special part to play in the final unity of men in the Church. So completely united to God herself, she is a symbol of that unity which men are to enjoy with their Lord. He put this thought thus: "When we . . . give to Our Blessed Mother the title of Our Lady of the Atonement, we mean, Our Lady of Unity. As she sits enthroned she represents to the universe the highest possible approach of a creature to intimate and exalted union with God . . . But Our Lady of the Atonement is not alone the Mother of God, she is also the New Eve, the Mother of Mankind. She is the center of that family unity which Christ prayed and willed might flourish among His Sons and Daughters of the Atonement."

He likewise pointed out that Mary is Mother not only of Catholics but of those separated from her Son. "When, therefore, we address the Blessed Virgin as Our Lady of the Atonement, we conceive her to be our Mother and we her Children. Nor, because we are Catholics do we assert that she is the Mother of Catholics only; she is the Mother of all the baptised, whether they be within the fold of Peter or belong to the 'other sheep' mentioned by the Good Shepherd, abroad in the desert places of heresy and schism, yet dear to Jesus and to the Mother heart of Mary."

Father Paul referred to the parable of the prodigal son and added that just as the father's heart went out to his son, so "we can conceive the Heart of Mary going out in yearning over her children who have wandered so far from the Holy Father's House, and from the Fold of Peter, the Universal Shepherd."

He used the same parable on another occasion with reference to Our Lady's part in bringing souls back to God. He said that the work of Unity would delight Our Lady. "Our Lord revealed the Father's love for the prodigal son and of course Mary's heart is a reflection of the Father's heart. Nothing is said about the mother at home, but she must have been praying for the wandering boy as well as the father and rejoicing with him at the feast and preparing the fatted calf, just as mothers usually prepare feasts today. So we can very well imagine what love and devotion Our Lady of the Atonement has for her wandering sheep, the heretics and schismatics, and she longs to bring them into union with Our Divine Lord, into one Fold, under one Shepherd."

Father Paul said that the work of the Society of the Atonement was to prepare the way as did St. John the Baptist, so that those souls outside the Church might readily enter. He mentioned the text from the breviary—*Guade Virgo Maria, cunctas haereses sola interemisiti in universo mundo*—"Rejoice O Virgin Mary, thou alone has destroyed all heresies through the world." Such was Father Paul's comment: "Our Lady has long been known as Destroyer of all Heresies; let her now be looked up to and invoked as the Mother who will not rest until her children, long estranged from each other as true brethren, and realizing the glorious fellowship of the one household of the faith, the answer to Our Divine Lord's prayer: 'That they all may be one as Thou, Father in Me and I in Thee, that they may be one in Us: that the world may believe that Thou has sent Me' ".

Father Paul then applied the text of the prophet Isaias to Mary: "it was of Our Lady of the Atonement that Isaias prophesied long ago under the inspiration of the Holy Ghost: 'They that be of thee shall build up the old waste places; thou shalt raise up the foundations of many generations; and thou shalt be called the repairer of the breach, the restorer of paths to dwell in'. (58:12). We have quoted this text in the version always used by Father Paul. In the Douay-Rheims translation we read: "The places that have been desolate for ages shall be built in thee, thou shalt raise up the foundations of generation and generation; and thou shalt be called the repairer of fences, turning the paths into rest." Actually the term "repairer of fences" does not seem to connote the same idea, though surely the words "The places that have been desolate for ages shall be built in thee" can be accommodated to the notion of Christian Unity, for the countries of Europe have been desolate for ages. But just as St. Augustine states that God would not permit evil if He could not draw forth a greater good, so we know that at some time these countries, once stripped of the faith and of devotion to the Mother of God, will return to their ancient heritage and to the glory they enjoyed when they saluted the Queen of heaven and earth as their beloved Mother.

We can again cite Father Paul's reference to Mary as Spouse of the Holy Spirit and her love for souls estranged from the Church, "Our Lady of the Atonement is herself the 'Seat of Wisdom'" as the Spouse of the Holy Ghost, and supported by countless legions of angels, we may rely on her maternal heart never to rest until the words of her Divine Son have been fulfilled: 'Other sheep have I which are not of this fold, them also I must bring and they shall hear my voice and there shall be One Fold and One Shepherd.'"

At the Shrine of Our Lady of the Atonement on the Convent Grounds (now also the tomb of Mother Lurana), Father Paul spoke of the unity aspect of Our Lady's place in the world (Feast of Our Lady, July 9, 1930) "There are many aspects any one of which we might use to treat the theme of Our Lady of the Atonement's title, but this morning we shall confine ourselves to that meaning of this New Name for the Blessed Virgin which sets forth her mission as Our Lady of Unity." He began by stating that the Latin title for Mary *Domina Nostra Adunationis,* gives the idea of Unity, that Our Lady cooperated with Christ in the salvation of the world by suffering at the foot of the

158

Cross, that the purpose of the Incarnation and Atonement was to "render infinite satisfaction for man's sins to the Divine Majesty and to bring man back to more than primal rectitude". Then he spoke of the disunity of Christendom; the Church is one, but there have been and are "vast lapses from the Fold". It is this "vast multitude outside the Unity of the Apostolic See (this Unity is the test of Catholicity) for whose return we must unceasingly invoke Our Lady of the Atonement, whom we call in her Litany 'Pillar of Unity' and 'Shepherdess of the Wandering Sheep'".

Father Paul showed how the word *adunare* is used in the Latin liturgy and returned to a plea to invoke Mary as "Our Lady of the Atonement ... Shepherdess of the Wandering Sheep and Pillar of Unity. Let us never doubt that by her powerful assistence, and with our cooperation, she will draw them back into unity with God and each other in the communion of the One, Holy, Catholic, Apostolic and Roman Church".

Then he turned to the theme of Mary in glory and said that she wears a robe of red in honor of the Precious Blood. "Let us look up to her, all radiant on her throne, apparelled in the crimson robe of the Precious Blood, interceding at this moment for the great At-one-ment; and may we never cease to unite our prayers with hers that the scales may fall away from the eyes of our separated brethren and that they may understand that Great Shepherd whom Our Lord has appointed as His Vice-regent on earth is *their* Father and *their* Shepherd."

Thus, as an Apostle of Unity, Father Paul chose for his special patron Our Blessed Lady under the title of the Atonement. To her he confided his joys and sorrows, his hopes and aspirations. Often he recited the rosary to pay tribute to her goodness and win grace for some soul. He rejoiced in all her feast days, the Immaculate Conception, the Nativity, the Assumption, the Feast of Our Lady of the

Rosary (also a community feast, Covenant Day) but most of all, the Feast of Our Lady of the Atonement. "This particular name of Our Blessed Mother is very dear to us," he said, "and we believe it is dear to Our Lady Herself. We hold it among the most treasured and sacred traditions of our Institute that it was the Blessed Virgin who first taught us to call her by that name and there are cogent reasons why she should give this title a favorite place among the many by which she is invoked".

Father Paul reasoned that just as Mary was completely united to God herself, so she was a most powerful intermediary for winning this unity for others. "It is recognized by all that this at-one-ment, or unity, between God and human creatures reaches its highest perfection and glory in the person of Our Lady of the Atonement herself, for she thereby has become the Daughter of God the Father, the Mother of God the Son, and Spouse of the Holy Ghost. It is in recognition of this intimate relationship of Our Blessed Mother with the Three Persons of the Holy Trinity that the Children of the Atonement are accustomed to address her by a Threefold Salutation."

The Threefold Salutation

When giving a retreat to the Sisters, the Graymoor Founder gave the following paraphrase and interpretation for the Threefold Salutation, which is the most frequently recited prayer to Our Lady in the Society of the Atonement, other than the Hail Mary. It was composed by Father Paul (and/or Mother Lurana) in the early days at Graymoor, about 1901. It is the direct prayer to Mary, the loving salutation of devoted children. It is a beautifully simple prayer that has received indulgences from the Holy See on several occasions.

The Threefold Salutation is an indulgenced prayer of

three hundred days (granted April 9, 1946) for the Friars and Sisters of the Atonement, the members of the Rosary League and of the Union-That-Nothing-Be-Lost. The original form was substantially the same as that used today; the only change is in the wording of the third salutation.

The original form of the prayer was as follows:

I salute thee, Holy Mary, Daughter of God the Father and entreat thee to obtain for us a devotion like thine own to the most sweet will of God.

I salute thee, Virgin Mother of God the Son and entreat thee to obtain for us such union with the Sacred Heart of Jesus that our own hearts may burn with love of God and an ardent zeal for the conversion of souls.

I salute thee, Immaculate Spouse of the Holy Ghost, and entreat thee to obtain for us the grace of an entire self-surrender to the inspiration and guidance of the Holy Spirit, that we may never grieve Him in thought, word or deed, but that He may, in all things, direct and rule our hearts. (*Rose Leaves* Nov. 1901)

Here we may present a brief commentary on the prayer from the writings of Father Paul.

I. *We salute thee Holy Mary, Daughter of God the Father and entreat thee to obtain for us a devotion like thine own to the most sweet will of God.* The explanation given was the following: "The first salutation is taking Our Lady's devotion as a pattern to the most sweet will of God, and there you have the beauty of obedience. If you want to hear God say in your souls what He said when St. John the Baptist was baptising Our Lord and again when Our Lord was transfigured on Mount Tabor: 'This is My beloved Son in Whom I am well pleased', you must worship the most sweet will of God. You must do everything from a supernatural motive because it is pleasing to God, because it makes you walk in the footsteps of Our Blessed Lady."

II. *We salute thee, Virgin Mother of God the Son and entreat thee to obtain for us such union with the Sacred Heart of Jesus that our own hearts may burn with love of God and an ardent zeal for the salvation of souls.* In this instance Father Paul turns to the Eucharist as the font of spiritual life. Our Lady is our Model and Guide in devotion to the Blessed Sacrament. "The second salutation is in regard to the devotion to Our Blessed Lord, devotion to His Sacred Heart so that our hearts may be united with His and, therefore, burning with love and charity and holy zeal for the conversion of sinners. Now all know that the center of the Sacred Heart, of course, is the Blessed Sacrament; it is of the Sacred Heart an outward and visible reminder, but the Heart Itself is in the tabernacle, and in our devotion to the Blessed Sacrament we are expressing in the best possible way our devotion to the Sacred Heart, union with the Sacred Heart. And so there is our second salutation, for Our Lady to pray for us and to cooperate with us in our devotion to Our Blessed Lord."

III. *We salute thee, Immaculate Spouse of God the Holy Ghost and entreat thee to obtain for us such yielding of ourselves to the Blessed Holy Spirit that He may in all things direct our hearts and that we may never grieve Him in thought, word or deed.* About this portion of the prayer Father Paul said: "The third salutation is one in regard to yielding ourselves to the Blessed Spirit, Who was the Spouse of Our Lady, and she of course, is the pattern of that devotion. And so, if you put behind that salutation your prayer, and commit it to Our Lady with the intention that is vital for every day, that you may realize in your religious

162

life, more and more, that union—and that At-one-ment with God the Father, God the Son, and God the Holy Ghost, it will be very wholesome and very effective. As far as your sanctification is concerned, I would recommend to you especially, to address Our Lady with the prayer to intercede for you to the Holy Ghost, the Sanctifier, in regard to your faults and your weaknesses and your defects, whatever they may be, embody them, more or less, in your confession, in your self-examination during this retreat, and I trust, in the resolutions you form for the future. Now take these resolutions to Our Lady and ask her to address them particularly to the Holy Ghost that He may strengthen and sanctify you and confirm your will in running more diligently the race that is set for you in the way of holy perfection. The more difficulty that you have in bringing your human nature to correspond to the divine nature of Our Lord, the greater will be your joy in the end."

The prayer was a favorite one with Father Paul. It expressed so simply and so well his trust and esteem in Our Lady. He lived his love of Our Lady in every way—as a priest, as a religious, as a man of prayer, and as an apostle of unity.

At times Father Paul spoke with unusual tenderness and insight about the title of Our Lady of the Atonement. Thus he asked the members of the Rosary League: "Did anyone else ever call you a Child of the Atonement except the writer of these letters?" And he went on to reply, giving his opinion as to its superlative importance. "Others have called you repeatedly, and you have called yourself—a Child of Mary—but a Child of the Atonement, never, perhaps. Yet it was by reason of the Atonement that the Blessed Virgin became your Mother and you became her Child. No words of mine can adequately describe the grandeur of Mary's Atonement Motherhood and the sublime dignity which has befallen us by virtue of our Atonement Birthright."

At another time, on Mother's Day, 1939, he explained what he meant by the title of Our Lady of the Atonement, and concluded with sentiments that he must often have experienced in his soul. "She is such a wonderful Mother!" he said, "how you ought to love her and how you ought to trust and invoke her, remembering that this beautiful Mother in heaven wishes her children to be pure and holy on earth and to obey God as she obeyed Him. So—let us not only cultivate a beautiful devotion to the Blessed Virgin, but strive ourselves to be saints, reflecting not only the image of Christ in our soul and His conduct in our life, but that of our altogether lovely Mother, the stainless one, the Queen of Heaven, and the consort of Jesus Christ upon His throne."

Father Paul said that the Holy Father had issued a *Motu proprio* in 1919 by which the young Society was permitted to celebrate the feast of Our Lady of the Atonement. He referred to the permission as a "great favor" and went on to say that he thought in time it would become a universal feast. "In time we have no doubt that the devotion to Our Lady under that title will extend to the Universal Church at large, because of the high significance of the title and its primacy in importance and what it must mean to Our Lady herself. We have no doubt that in time to come it will be celebrated by the whole Church throughout the world. We started in 1908 at Graymoor the Chair of Unity Octave, when we were very small. It has spread throughout the Universal Church, but it is also observed by many thousands among our separated brethren—and we feel that this devotion will spread far and wide. Let us think this morning of the title and how precious it must be to the Blessed Virgin herself." Since 1948, the feast of Our Lady of the Atonement on July 9 has enjoyed papal approval for the Friars and Sisters of the Atonement. This is the patronal feast of the Rosary League directed by the Atonement Sisters. It is the feast day for the members of the League of Prayer for Unity under the patronage of Our Lady of the Atonement, given papal approval in 1956. It now has one hundred and eighty thousand members who pray daily for Unity. This pious union is directed by the Friars as a development of the Chair of Unity Octave.

It seems that Father Paul thought that the title of Our Lady of the Atonement and devotion to her under that name would be propagated through the Unity Octave and spread to all parts of the world. In all the houses of the Society, in Italy, Ireland, Japan, and the United States and Canada, the Madonna of Graymoor, Our Lady of the Atonement, is honored by her Atonement Sons and Daughters with affection and devotion. It is remarkable that the name and devotion were approved so early in the history of the Community, and particularly since the Founders of the Society were members of the Church less than ten years when the privilege was given by the Holy See.

There is one point that Father Founder brought out in his last talk on the Feast of Our Lady of the Atonement (July 9, 1939). He said that the title of Our Lady of the Atonement does not mean only that the Blessed Virgin stood by the Cross, or suffered with Christ, but that her name also embraces the concept of joy, the joy of the redeemed who has attained at-one-ment with God for all eternity. Sorrow is temporal; but joy is eternal. This was his idea:

> I daresay Our Lady values with different degrees the titles that are given her in the Litany of Loretto, and I am satisfied that there is none of them that appeals to her more than that of the Atonement. One of the incidents connected with the Atonement was sor-

row, for though she brought forth her first-born Son in Bethlehem with joy, Mary had to travail with sorrow in bringing the children of the Atonement, because they were conceived in sin and this new birth in God involved the very death of the Redeemer of the world. All the sorrows of Our Lady, by perfect sympathy, were expressed in the heart of Mary. Our Lord, in death, was pierced by a spear and her heart was pierced by a sword of anguish. But sorrow was incidental. It was not the great thing of the Atonement, even as Our Lord said in one of the addresses to the Apostles before He took His departure from them: 'In a little while you shall not see Me because I go to the Father. Your sorrows are for a little while; while your souls are eternal . . . A woman when she is in travail hath sorrow but when the child is born, she remembreth no more the sorrow because of the joy that a son is born into the world'. So the sorrows of the Blessed Virgin are transitory. They are not permanent, but the joy that comes to her through the Atonement, that is eternal. In sorrow she brings forth the Children of the Atonement but when that is passed she forgets the sorrow when the Children of the Atonement are brought into the kingdom of God in eternal glory."

Father Paul's love of Our Lady of the Atonement manifested itself in his words to the laity. He would ask them, on her feast day, to celebrate it by wearing a medal of Our Lady of the Atonement with red ribbon, in honor of the Most Precious Blood. He urged them whenever possible to observe the feast by being "present at Mass and receiving Holy Communion" and if this were impossible, then to go to Confession on Saturday "so as to be cleansed in the Precious Blood of the Atonement, and partake, on Sunday morning, the Body of Christ, as an act of pure devotion to His Immaculate Mother, and ours, by virtue of His Cross and Atoning Sacrifice." He suggested that at home the laity make it a "feast day by placing flowers on Our Lady's altar and burning votive lights, and . . . give the family a specially good dinner in Our Lady's honor." Father Paul told of his joy in the development of the Rosary League: "We rejoice in the growth of the Rosary League and of the increasing devotion of its members to our Blessed Mother under the beautiful title of Mary of the Atonement. The ever-growing list of testimonials of favors granted through the Novena of Last Resort is evidence that the Blessed Virgin is pleased with the love and confidence we repose in her and is exercising her intercessory power with God in behalf of the Children of the Atonement."

The previous pages have not given a complete treatment of Father Paul's devotion to the Mother of God, for they are meant only to serve as an outline of his devotion to and spiritual teaching of Mary as Our Lady of the Atonement. He emphasized the fact that Mary cooperated in a unique way in the sacrifice of Unity, the mystery of the Cross, that she continues her mission of unity by applying the merits of her Son, of obtaining grace for the souls of men, so that the effects of the Atonement are perpetuated throughout the whole Mystical Body of Christ. Mary continues the ministry of At-*one*-ment by being the means whereby heresy is overcome and souls enter the Church, achieving union with the Divine Trinity in this life which is a prelude to the unending bliss of paradise. Mary is not the agent of grace, but its instrument; grace passes through her—through her mediation, her intercession, her prayer, her love. Man's individual desires and petitions may be sordid indeed, but once they have received the acceptance of Mary, then they seem to take on a different aspect. For how can the loving Son refuse such a Mother as Mary? And so in the Catholic faith there is no doctrine so consoling, so heartening, so rewarding, so filled with blessed strength and spiritual courage, as the truth that Mary is *Mater Dei et Mater Mei*—the Mother of God and my Mother.

And so this title for the Mother of God, originated by the beloved Founders of Graymoor, emphasizing Mary's participation in the mystery of the Atonement and her role in the tremendous enterprise of Christian Unity, is indeed a source of joy and love for the members of the Society. It places upon them the duty to make Mary known, loved and venerated as a holy obligation which they gladly and generously assume. A Mother of such love deserves the best efforts of her children.

Mary is the glory of heaven, the joy of the angels, the mistress of the world. She is the incomparable woman; she will overcome all the powers of separation and division and bring the entire universe into that harmony of peace and love which is a reflection of the Unity and blessedness of the Divine Trinity. Those who know the power and love of Mary will appreciate the following thoughts from the writings of Cardinal Suenens of Brussels:

> In this immense struggle all the forces of God must unite for the salvation of humanity. That is why, no doubt, the Church is experiencing at present, with renewed keenness, a longing for the return of our separated brethren of her unity. This problem dominates all others; now or never is the time to remember that Jesus Himself bound up Christian unity with belief in his mission—*Ut sint unum!* "That they all may be one, as Thou Father in Me, and I in Thee—that the world may believe that Thou hast sent Me."
>
> Frequently in history attempts have been made to resolve this problem by learned skillful discussions;

often they have brought bitterness into differences; they have never achieved lasting results.

Here again it seems that Mary's hour has come. When children have left their home and no longer understand one another, does not the memory of their tenderly loved mother remain the strongest link between them and the best hope of seeing the family reconciled?

Mary is a mother like no other; she is the warmth of the home. She calls her children to press themselves against her heart. Close to her they will realize how much they are brothers, one of another.

Return to the unity of the Church through return to the common love of Mary. What a wonderful dream! Why should it be forbidden to believe that rivalry in active devotion towards Our Lady will one day reunite our separated brethren? It would be a task greatly after a mother's heart. Is that Utopian? Not at all, for Marian devotion, which is finding among Anglicans willing expression and is returning to certain Protestant groups, has remained vigorous and profound in the immense world of the East with Russia as its principal stronghold.

Mary offers herself as the connecting link between Eastern and Western Christianity. She is a common blessing, a priceless treasure, passionately beloved. Let us each, then, open his soul to her that she may take possession of it. Mary will lead her children with a sure and gentle hand to the one fold where the whole truth is to be found, the fullness of life, Jesus Christ, Our Lord.

Father Paul believed strongly in the power of the Immaculate Virgin. He was certain that just as in the past centuries Mary overcame the forces of the enemy which were attacking the Church with military might, so in the present age when Christ is attacked in His Church by the enemies of truth, peace and love, and the ranks of those who profess to be His followers are divided more than ever, then Mary will unite and bring back to the Church those groups separated from the One Body of the Divine Redeemer. For in the words of Father Paul: "Who so much as Our Lady of the Atonement might be expected to propagate and extend an association—specially devoted to the Unity of the One Fold and salvation through His Atoning Blood of the heathen world?" ... "Only the Eve of the New Covenant, the Queen of the Holy Rosary, as we use her personally bestowed prayer, petitioning the mercy of God, shall bring about the solution of that condition expressed in the words of St. Peter, the Prince of the Apostles, when he said: ' ... there were also false prophets among the people, even as there shall be among you lying teachers who shall bring in sects of perdition, and deny the Lord who brought them, bringing upon themselves swift destruction.' "

Father Paul called attention to Mary's great longing to have all men united in the One Church of God, "Mary is the New Eve," he declared. "She is the Mother of the regenerate, of all those who live for God in Christ Jesus; the Sons and Daughters of the Atonement. Vast as the number of these children have become, they are not sufficient to satisfy the maternal heart of Mary. She will not be satisfied until all the children of Eve, dwelling upon the face of the earth in all parts of the world, have been born again into the Kingdom of Heaven and are numbered among the elect Children of the Atonement."

The present text of the Mass and Office of our Lady of the Atonement combines the two ideas of Calvary and Unity. Some of the Mass is taken from the feast of our Lady of Sorrows (Sept. 15) while other parts are from the votive Mass for the Unity of the Church. For example, the Introit begins with the words of St. John "now there stood

170

by the Cross of Jesus Mary his Mother." Then the oration is a prayer for unity:

O God, Who dost gather together those who have been scattered and who dost preserve those who have been gathered together: we beseech Thee through the intercession of the Most Blessed Virgin Mary Thou wilt pour out upon Thy Church the grace of Unity.

The office is for the most part taken from the common of Our Lady, though the lessons for the second nocturn are the same as those for the feast of our Lady's Sorrows. Both texts use the ideas that Father Paul and Mother Lurana advanced in their devotion to Our Lady of the Atonement. Other prayers have been approved by the Holy See, such as the litany of our Lady of the Atonement, and the consecration to her for use of the Graymoor Friars and Sisters.

Thus in the Providence of Almighty God, Father Paul of Graymoor was not only an Apostle of Unity in the twentieth century, or a modern Poverello by his joyful adherence to the Franciscan spirit of holy poverty for the love of God, but he was a most devoted Son of Mary, confident of her intercession in all his trials and difficulties, plans and projects. Mother Lurana used to speak of his great love for the Mother of God, Our Lady of the Atonement. It was such love that gave him that loyalty to the Church, that love of Christ and that zeal for the salvation of souls that characterized his entire life. If Father Paul is known for his unity vocation, for his compassion for the outcast, for his love of St. Francis and all that Seraphic spirit means, he should equally and justifiably be known as the religious Founder, passionately devoted to the cause of Christian Unity through Mary's intercession. Above all, he should be recognized as the originator of a Marian title and a devotion that he cherished so deeply.

Father Paul saw his vocation of Unity through the radiance of the Mother of God: "It has profoundly impressed us that our mission is not only to preach Christ Crucified, but also to promote and extend devotion to Our Lady of the Atonement ... until a vast number of the faithful shall be united with the Blessed Virgin, our Mother in heaven, in the work of prayer and intercession for the conversion of the whole world to Christ, so that the Passion and Atoning Sacrifice of our Divine Redeemer may be made effectual to the fullest extent in the salvation of souls and in the completion of God's elect."

His favorite image of Our Lady of the Atonement is the painting in St. Francis Chapel, Graymoor, wrought by Mother Margaret Mary Nealis, a Madame of the Sacred Heart in Montreal. This was executed in 1933. Our Lady wears the red mantle in honor of the Precious Blood and holds the Infant in her arms; He is the Child of the Atonement and has a cross in His right hand. Four angels bear the instruments of the Atonement by which men were made at-one with God. A copy of this work forms the frontispiece of this book. But the first painting of the Atonement Madonna was done in Rome in 1925 by G. Martini; it is somewhat Byzantine in style. The original representation was a statue made in 1901 and placed in Our Lady of the Angels Chapel, Graymoor. It is there today, a precious reminder of the veneration of a Marian apostle and of the tender kindness of a Mother who selected a loving son outside the Church to honor her as patroness of Christian Unity. Then she led him within, to the unity of the One Fold. A medal of Our Lady was first cast in 1905 and is still widely used. It is another token of the love of Mary for her children and of their burning affection for her.

Seven ◈ Epilogue

"Deign that I may be worthy to praise thee, O most Holy
Virgin."   —Roman Liturgy.

This treatise on Our Lady and Reunion is by no means
complete or adequate. It falls far short of what we desire
to write and immeasureably short of what might be said
of Our Lady. But we take consolation in the words of St.
Alphonsus Liguori, if one may dare to place himself along-
side so holy and so learned a man, when he wrote in his
introduction to the *Glories of Mary*: "Since the devotion that
led me to write and moves you to read this book makes us
both happy children of the same good Mother, should you
ever hear it said that I might well have spared myself the
labor, as there are already so many famous and learned
works on the same subject, I beg that you will answer in
the words of Abbot Francone that 'the praise of Mary is
an inexhaustible fountain, the more it is enlarged the fuller
it becomes, and the more you fill it, so much more is it
enlarged'. In short, the Blessed Virgin is so great and so
sublime that the more she is praised the more there is to
praise, so much so, as St. Augustine declares, 'if all the
tongues of men were put together, if each of their members
were changed into a tongue, they would not suffice to
praise her as she deserves.'"

It is our hope and desire—our fondest dream—that devotion to Our Lady for the cause of Unity will spread to all parts of the world. It is our prayer that interest in and love for the Mother of God under this beautiful concept will extend to all parts of the universe, making men more conscious of her role in their salvation and in the whole mission of the Church. In the political, economic, and social realm, men speak of the "One World" as kind of a Utopian dream, glorious in concept, but never to be realized. It is a goal which no one can reach, an illusion which attracts but can never satisfy because it is not real. But in the spiritual order this ideal can become a reality. Barriers of race, class, culture and position are dissolved into the higher unity of the Mystical Body, and they disappear in the all-embracing love of the Mother of God and the Mother of all men. The "One World" in spiritual terms is the family of God, the Catholic Church.

Devotion to Our Lady is not an appendage to the spiritual life, a spiritual luxury which men may use or not as they please. Love for Mary is important and necessary in the lives of all people, for the place of the Virgin Mother in the designs of God cannot be ignored or minimized. Love of Mary is a necessary counterpart of love for Jesus; love of Mary is intimately associated with man's salvation. In the words of Cardinal Montini of Milan: "True devotion to Mary is of such nature that, restored where necessary to its purposes, it may fulfill its proper function of leading us to Jesus by means of a most sincere, full and loving transformation of the old self into the new man of Justice and Christian sanctity. Every other form of Marian piety not oriented in this way will inevitably be deficient and less pleasing to the Heavenly Mother to whose heart nothing is dearer than our renewal in the life of her divine Son.'

"There is no need," he continues, "to speak about the precious fruits that would come to each and all within the

174

Church if this powerful influence of love for Mary which gives to our troubled times its brightest note of confidence were formed and disciplined according to the spirit of liturgical worship. Our relations to the Virgin, far from being exhausted in superficial sentimentality or in anxious and self-interested pleading for help in moments of need, would thereby acquire that character of maturity and depth so necessary for perseverance in the spiritual life."

As the years move on, the power of intercession, the love and kindness of Mary become increasingly evident and the attention of the faithful in all parts of the world is focused more clearly upon the masterpiece of God's love for her role in the spiritual life of men. Mary gave birth to all men in the agony of Calvary, as Pope Leo XIII declared: "It is thus that the crown of the kingdom of heaven and earth await her because she is the invincible Queen of Martyrs; it is thus that she is seated in the heavenly city of God by the side of her Son, crowned for all eternity, because she has drunk with Him the cup overflowing with sorrow, faithfully through all her life, most faithfully on Calvary."

And so we ask Our Blessed Lady, standing valiantly by the Cross of Her beloved Son, sharing His sacrifice, burning with love, to grant us an appreciation of the mystery of Calvary, to inspire us to share in some way in the great Act of the Atonement so as to become co-heirs with Christ and with His Mother in their glory.

We think of the influence of Our Lady through all the centuries, in the catacombs, in the glorious fourth century of the Church, in the so-called Dark Ages, in the golden era of the thirteenth century, in the years of the Protestant revolt, and finally up to the modern scientific world. But throughout all history the image of Mary is there, sometimes in the background, at other times in the foreground. Her presence cannot be ignored. For Our Lady is

175

too much a part of the history of the Church and of the world to be eclipsed from view. Or, as the writer M. Dosset has declared: "The Virgin Mother evokes in us heroic efforts and manly aspirations. From her proceed directly the flames that fire our apostles, the devotion of our admirable religious in all the battle-fields of zeal, the faith of the humble, and the constancy of the martyrs. No one could count the acts of valor that she has sustained and the hopes that she has aroused. How many men have remained alive through the aid of her prayers alone; how many lost souls have escaped death because of her arms . . . Let the one who is able measure the immense abyss and the desolution created by the absence of this star in the midst of Protestantism."

We hope that this book is only a beginning. It is indeed a matter of bricks and mortar; the superstructure is still to be erected. The walls and the roof, the embellishments of stone and stained glass, the majestic tower to crown all efforts—these are the work for the future. We hope that our modest contribution on Our Lady and Reunion will help towards an understanding of her role as the Great Mother of the world, praying for all men. The renowned scholar Scheeben could say that "As Christ is the Father of the new race through His suffering . . . so Mary is the Mother of the same race through participation in His Passion." And again: "As the Bride of God conceiving and bearing Him, she is therefore chosen and qualified to cooperate in His work of redemption."

Thus it is always, as ordained by God from all eternity: Christ and Mary, the Saviour and Our Lady, the King and Queen, the Son and His Mother. Mary is no obstacle to the love of Christ. She is a necessary way to Him, necessary because God in His goodness and wisdom has willed it so.

Our Lady of the Atonement, Mother of Unity, pray for us!